D0800641

THE
MANDRAKE

BY NICCOLÒ MACHIAVELLI
TRANSLATED BY WALLACE SHAWN

★

★

DRAMATISTS
PLAY SERVICE
INC.

THE MANDRAKE was first presented by the New York Shakespeare Festival (Joseph Papp, producer) at the Public Theater, in New York City, in November, 1977. It was directed by Wilford Leach; the set design was by Mr. Leach; costumes were by Patricia McGourty; music was by Richard Weinstock; the lighting was by Victor En Yu Tan; and the painting was done by set design associate Bob Shaw. The associate producer was Bernard Gersten, and the production stage manager was Bill McComb. The cast, in order of appearance, was as follows:

SINGER .... Thelma Nevitt

PROLOGUE & SIRO .... Wallace Shawn

CALLIMACO .... James Lally

LIGURIO .... John Ferraro

PROFESSOR NICIA .... Tom Costello

WAITER .... Paca Thomas

MADONNA SOSTRATA .... Angela Pietropinto

BROTHER TIMOTHY .... Larry Pine

WOMAN AT THE CHURCH ....Angela Pietropinto

MADONNA LUCREZIA .... Corinne Fischer

Scene: Florence, Italy.

3

FOREWORD

The Mandrake can be seen as a dark, grotesque play or a sunny, delicious one; it is arguably a cruel satire or a joyful tract in praise of human behavior—harsh or kindly, disturbing or delightful, depending on one's point of view. Many interpretations are possible, and many sorts of productions are possible.

As a piece for performance, it may be very well done either simply or elaborately. Indeed, one of the nice things about *The Mandrake* is that it may be performed with no more scenery than a simple backdrop (and indeed, even that may easily be dispensed with). The costumes can be simple suggestions of character, either in a sixteenth century style or not, as one pleases, and the songs—which were added by Machiavelli after the play had already been written and performed without them—may be omitted, or sung by a single voice to a simple accompaniment of keyboard or guitar. On the other hand, the background of Renaissance Florence makes the play quite suitable for an opulent treatment, with gorgeous costumes and splendid scenery—and a large chorus of nymphs and shepherds backed by a varied ensemble of appealing instruments. The style of performance may be severe or casual, naturalistic or caricatured, farcical or witty, intellectual or passionate. And the characters too are subject to all sorts of interpretations. In any case, I have included very few stage directions in the text, in order to allow directors, designers, and actors the greatest possible degree of interpretive liberty.

At the end of the text, I have included a note on the already legendary production of *The Mandrake* directed by Wilford Leach at Joseph Papp's New York Shakespeare Festival Public Theater. This was the first production to use this translation, and a few words describing it may serve as an inspiration to those who are now planning to put on this play.

4

A NOTE ON THE TRANSLATION

In case you're curious, the basic facts about the translation are these:

1. About twelve per cent of the material in my original translation has been cut for this performing edition. The cuts more or less correspond to those made for the Wilford Leach production, although they have been modified so as to suit, in my opinion, all different sorts of productions. The play is definitely better without the extra twelve per cent; it is now just long enough, and not too long, and little of importance has been lost.

2. Before the cuts were made, every line (speech) of the translation corresponded to a line (speech) of the original, and each line of the translation had more or less the same meaning as the original line.

3. The *way* the meaning of the line was conveyed was pretty much up to me. If a simple line in English didn't have the significance, or the strength, of Machiavelli's simple line, I wrote a longer line in English. If the meaning of some line in the original could not be understood unless I put in a few extra sentences in the translation, I just put them right in, or if the *feeling* of the Italian took a few extra words to convey, I cheerfully added these as well. Somehow, for every week I spent translating the play from Italian into literal English, I ended up spending three weeks turning my literal English into the translation you now have in your hands.

4. The original play is surprising and powerful and alive. My guiding principle was to try to translate this spirit, to enable the play to live for us today as it lived for those who saw it when it was first written and performed.

CAST OF CHARACTERS

CALLIMACO, *a nobleman of Florence:*
Callimaco is thirty years old. He's not a very serious young man. He's wealthy and charming, and he is in the most charming way completely obsessed with himself. As far as he's concerned, the only important thing in the world is his own state of satisfaction. He expects the world to be sad when's he's sad, happy when he's happy. He has a powerful need for everyone to like him, and, as far as he knows, everyone does, and this pleases him. He doesn't need to work, and so his life can center around whims and passions.

SIRO, *Callimaco's servant:*
Siro has served Callimaco for ten years. He really could be any age himself. He's more worldly than Callimaco; he knows more about how things work. The basic fact about him is that he has no life of his own; his life is just an instrument to be used by his master; he therefore represents a stunted, degraded form of humanity, despite his intelligence. He actually loves Callimaco and wants to protect him. In the context of his small, mean life, it is fun for him to put on a disguise and fool Lord Nicia; he doesn't take himself seriously enough to adopt an ethical position on any issue, even in his own mind, although of all the characters he may be the one most capable of moral awareness.

LIGURIO, *a man who lives by his wits:*
Ligurio is probably in his thirties, although he could be older. He is a poor man who lives among the rich. The rich live in a dream of passion; they have no need to be intelligent, and so they aren't. Ligurio earns his living from his intelligent and accurate observation of the rich. The rich are deluded by passions, and he has none, except the passion to survive. Undeluded by emotions himself, he uses the emotions of the rich for his own gain. He is obsequious when it is necessary, not when it is not necessary. He knows how to appeal to each different sort of person: some want to be flattered, some want friendship, and some will take a bribe quite happily without the need for any personal exchange. Ligurio's life is an exhausing one, lived among those for whom life is easy. About his personal situation and feelings, we can only speculate; what does he go home to?

6

Lord Nicia, *husband of Lucrezia:*
Lord Nicia could be in his forties, or he could be older. He is a lawyer and scholar of law (like Machiavelli's father). He's not very happy. Although he has money of his own and so doesn't need clients, he seems not to be respected in Florence as a lawyer, and it's clear he's not respected as a man. The truth is that everyone finds him slow and uninteresting and somehow repellent, and no one really likes him, and surely he must know that this is so. Like Callimaco, the other wealthy and well-born character, he is absorbed in his own desperate passion— in his case, his desire for a son, into which he has poured all his hopes and all his dreams. He seems to see his wife as an infuriating failure, because they have had no children, and he speaks of her usually in a cold and sour manner. He is very much alone in the world, embittered and distant.

Brother Timothy, *a friar:*
Brother Timothy could be in his thirties, his forties, or older. He obviously enjoys the things that money can buy, and he enjoys his own intelligence and skill at persuasion. He seems to have absolutely no feelings, but this may not be the case. He clearly remembers with nostalgia the life of simple piety that once existed and that he himself perhaps once shared in. He may even have some sense of self-disgust, and regret for what he has become. He is clearly a man of brilliance. At times he may derive pleasure from the very fact of his coldness. At times he may feel a sense of emptiness and despair. We don't know about his private life; he seems to loathe women, and to be attracted to them.

Madonna Sostrata, *Lucrezia's mother:*
Madonna Sostrata is probably in her forties. She always wanted money, and now she has it. She has a reputation for being cheap and vulgar despite her wealth, and perhaps she doesn't mind this. She clearly knows Lord Nicia is no fun for her daughter, and she probably finds him quite irritating herself. Is it possible that she's interested in Brother Timothy? They certainly work well as a team. At any rate, she feels quite at home in the company of men. She undoubtedly enjoys a frivolous life of gossip, parties, and social visiting.

The Woman In The Church, *a widow:*
This character, who could really be of any age, represents a sort of uncorrupted life, a sensuality that has not become decadent. And yet she is enslaved by her own ignorance, and gives away her money foolishly to Brother Timothy, who has only contempt for her. Obviously she enjoys talking with him and perhaps is quite attracted to

7

him. She represents the only intrusion of ordinary life into an otherwise totally self-contained story, and as such she provides a background against which the very particular concerns of the other characters may be seen in greater relief.

MADONNA LUCREZIA, *the wife of Lord Nicia:*

Madonna Lucrezia is in her early twenties, and she is indeed a classic victim of society. She actually believes in the moral principles which society professes to believe in but does not. In order to obtain her subjugation and obedience, her mentors instructed her in morality; but now that their plans for her involve the rejection of all scruples, she enrages them by stubbornly adhering to the tenets she learned from them. Her resistance really is extraordinary and heroic: not only is she utterly alone in the sense that everyone else in her world is bent on her submission to a sickening rape; she is also spiritually alone, in that, in order to resist, she must believe in her own conscience over and against family, church, and all other opinion. Of course she has no choice in the end but to submit, because she has absolutely no power, no weapons, and nowhere to turn; even suicide is forbidden to her by the religion she adheres to. Her final transformation may be seen in many ways— as the story of how a person becomes corrupt, or makes the best of life; or as the story of some sort of divine redemption. Perhaps Machiavelli is actually saying, shocking as it may be to believe this, that evil leads to good.

THE MANDRAKE

(*Enter two nymphs and two shepherds, who proceed to sing.*)

Life
on
this earth
is very short,
many
are
the pains
that,
living
and
struggling,
each person
sustains—
that is why
we,
following
our whim,
have left the daily world
of noisy strife
to pursue the life
of shepherds
and nymphs,
passing and using up the years
in frivolities
in play,
because he
who deprives himself of pleasure
to live in anguish
and breathless
despair
in the ordinary world
must either

somehow
be insensible
to the anguish he suffers
himself,
and the evils
the strange events
by which almost all mortals are oppressed,
almost all are oppressed,
or else he must be blind
to the ways
by which
he might escape them.
Now we—
who have chosen
in our secluded spots
to flee from
the weariness of the world
frolicking in festivity and joy
young
comely
happy youths
and light-hearted nymphs
forever—
we have come
with our harmony
here
on a rare
visit,
to pay our respects
to you who've stayed behind,
to honor this pleasant
occasion
the making of a play
and your sweet company,
and to amuse ourselves by watching
this story of the world we've left
and the people
still in it.

(An actor speaks the Prologue.)

Good evening, everyone. And if you're glad to be here, well then let me say, God bless you! (*Pause*.) Now tonight we're going to show you something really rather strange—yes, it's a sort of a strange incident that happened in the city of Florence, in Italy; this will be the subject of our play. And this, as you can very well see, is the set. Now for tonight, it represents Florence. But on another occasion, we might use the very same set to represent Rome, or Pisa, or any other city—and that's what we call "the magic of the theatre." It really is. Now, this doorway here—this represents the house of a scholar of law, a learned man—and this road here we call the Road of Love; and they say that if you stumble along the Road of Love, you will never rise again. Then, further along in the play, you'll be able to see what sort of a father-confessor, clothed in a friar's habit, lives in that church over there. And then here we have the home of a young man whose name is Callimaco, and he's just returned to Florence after having lived for many, many years in the city of Paris; and he's generally considered by his neighbors to be a very fine fellow. And you see, there was a certain very clever young woman who was very greatly loved by this same young man, and because of this she was the victim of a bizarre and cruel trick, as you will very soon see. It was very cruel and very bizarre, but it's my sincere wish all the same that you, too, could somehow be tricked in a similar fashion—

And so we have before us—a lover; a pedant; and a corrupt friar; —and then, in the second scene, a scheming parasite. These make up our evening's entertainment.

And if this frivolous material seems unworthy of a writer and a man who would like to be taken seriously, who would like to be considered to be a person who might just possibly have something important to offer to the world—you may say he wrote this pitiful and silly little play simply to make his dull, unhappy days pass a bit more pleasantly. He has no other recourse, no choice, you see, because all other doors have been repeatedly slammed

11

in his face, and the opportunity to show in more important types of work his more valuable talents has been consistently denied him, there being no respect paid to him and no reward offered for the years of dedication he has given to the world.

The reward that he expects this evening is that each one of you will sit in your little seat and sneer at his play, ripping to shreds in your minds every line and every scene. And of course that's the most common thing in the world today. Everyone loves to criticize and destroy. But unfortunately the consequence of this tendency is that artistic activity happens to be dying out in our world today; and the end result of this is that our world is growing very ugly and debased; because do you really think that the few people of talent who are alive today are going to spend their hours ripping their guts out and smashing their heads against walls trying to produce works of art? Well, they certainly are not, because they know very well that the work that they produce will immediately be torn to bits by gales of envious and ignorant vituperation, or else—what is even worse—it will be instantly buried by a thick and sickly fog of total neglect.

But if those who sit carping and criticizing think that they have this author by the hair, if they think that they can shut him up or frighten him, or keep him in his place, then let me warn them; let me tell them that he too knows how to use words to destroy his fellow human beings, and indeed this was a talent which he possessed before he had any other, and in the entire world he is in awe of no one, even though he may act very polite and deferential, very respectful and submissive, to those who are more "important" than he is, and even though he may crawl down and kiss the feet of those whose lovely clothes are more fashionable and expensive than his own.

But let those who wish to criticize go right ahead and do so. Let *us* turn to our story. Time is getting on, so let's forget everything I said. Callimaco is coming out of his house, and with him is his servant, Siro, and Callimaco's first few lines will make all the background clear. So let's all pay attention to the play, and expect no further comment from me tonight.

ACT ONE

SCENE 1

(*Callimaco and Siro.*)

CALLIMACO. Don't go, Siro. I need you a bit longer.

SIRO. I'm here, master.

CALLIMACO. Siro, I have to talk to you. We haven't spoken much recently, and I wanted to explain— Now I'm sure you found it odd, the way we left Paris—so suddenly—and you must have assumed I had something very urgent to do here in Florence. —But here we are, and we've been here a month, and I haven't done a thing! You must find it very puzzling—

SIRO. Well, Sir, I do—

CALLIMACO. I know I've kept certain things to myself—it's not that I don't trust you. You know I don't tell anyone my business if I don't want the whole world to know it, and I don't make any exceptions unless I'm forced to. But I'm going to need your help, so I'm ready to tell you the entire story.

SIRO. Sir— I'm your servant; and servants should not put questions to their masters, or try to understand what their masters do. When their masters decide to speak to *them*, then they must serve them faithfully; and this I have done, and will continue to do.

CALLIMACO. I know it. But now listen to my tale. I'll have to begin with my childhood in order to explain it. And I know you've heard about my childhood a thousand times, but it's very important, so you're going to hear about it again once more. You remember I was only ten years old—and my parents, my mother and my father, were both dead—they were *dead*—when my tutors arranged to send me away from my home, here in Florence, all the way to Paris, where I ended up staying for the next twenty years. I might have come back when I reached the age of twenty, but just at that moment—because of those God-damned expeditions of King Carlo the Eighth—war broke out suddenly, all over Italy; when I learned that the province of my birth had been hopelessly destroyed, I vowed I would live forever in Paris and never think of coming home again.

SIRO. Yes— I remember—

CALLIMACO. And those years in Paris were so carefree and delightful—

SIRO. Yes—they were great—

CALLIMACO. —I divided my time between pleasures and studies and my business affairs, and everyone I met just liked me so much —the most powerful lords, and the most miserable beggars and slaves— I was always so helpful and pleasant. —And I was always so careful not ever to offend or cause trouble, but always to please—

SIRO. Oh it's so true, Sir—

CALLIMACO. But Fortune thought my days were too sunny and too pleasant, and so she sent a certain man to come into my life— one Camillo Calfucci—

SIRO. Oh—

CALLIMACO. Like all Florentines in Paris, he was often at my house, and one day a group of us expatriates were talking, and we started to argue about whether French girls were really more appealing and beautiful than the girls in Italy, and the debate went on for quite a long time, and then Calfucci suddenly exclaimed that even if all other Italian women should be hideous beasts, there was a relative of his who could win the prize for Italy entirely on her own.

SIRO. Oh— Sir . . .

CALLIMACO. The person he named was Madonna Lucrezia, a woman of Florence, the wife of Lord Nicia Calfucci. Suddenly he was speaking about the beauty of her body and her face—and the intoxicating quality of her movements and gestures; everyone there was reduced to silence, each one sitting and staring blankly into the space in front of him. —I sat there too. The wars in Italy no longer seemed important. A desire to see this woman stood up, stood up violently, in my heart. I decided to depart. I made my plans, and I left. When I arrived in Florence, I was greeted by a rare discovery: the girl's beauty in fact is infinitely greater than what Calfucci could convey in words. And now I find myself here, but I'm so obsessed by the desire to have sexual relations with this woman that I'm weak, ill, and dizzy, and I don't know where I am. (*Pause.*)

SIRO. If you'd told me about this in Paris, Sir, I would have known just how to advise you; but now—well, I really don't know what to say.

14

CALLIMACO. I didn't tell you all this because I want your advice —I had to express these *feelings!* —don't you see that I'm dying? And I want you to begin to prepare yourself to serve me, to help me, to do whatever it is that will need to be done.

SIRO. I'm more than prepared already—you know that very well. But what hope do you have in this matter, Sir?

CALLIMACO. Oh God! God! I don't have any hope!

SIRO. Oh, master—

CALLIMACO. My very greatest obstacle is the girl's own nature. She has an extraordinary nobility of character, and she's completely uninterested in flirtation, love, or sex. She has an extremely rich husband who submits himself utterly to her every slightest wish, and while he's really quite old, he still seems to have enough blood in his veins to function as a husband. And she sees no one else—she never goes out to soirées or occasions or pleasant afternoons with neighbors or friends—

SIRO. Well—master—er—

CALLIMACO. But Siro, there are two things that do seem to be in my favor.

SIRO. Really?

CALLIMACO. Yes. The first is the simplicity of Lord Nicia, her husband—truly the most futile and pathetic man in Florence— "not smart, though a scholar," if you've heard that phrase. The second is the desire that he and his wife both have to have children. They've been married for six years; she's never conceived, they're very rich, and they have no heir, and the situation is making them both quite desperate. And there's a third point, in fact; the girl's mother was really—well—quite a cheap person in her day— really something of a whore—money used to attract her; but now she's rich, and I don't really know how I ought to approach her, but she could be very helpful in some way, I think—

SIRO. Oh— I see—

CALLIMACO. And there's one thing more. You know that— person—Ligurio—who's come over for so many meals in the last few days. He lives by eating at other people's houses; he arranges things; he used to arrange marriages at one time— Well, he has a very ingratiating manner, and people are somehow attracted to him, and I found out not long ago that Lord Nicia had taken him up rather recently and formed some sort of a close relationship with him. Anyway— I've managed to make myself a friend of this person—this Ligurio—and I've told him all about my passion, and he's promised to use all his many skills to help me.

SIRO. Sir—please be careful that this man doesn't attempt to betray you. These parasites—these professional gourmets—oh Sir, they can be utterly faithless.

CALLIMACO. I know that, of course. But I've promised this Ligurio a large sum of money if we're successful in this business. And if we fail—well, he'll get a few more meals. In any case, I don't mind eating with Ligurio. I'd rather eat with him than eat by myself.

SIRO. But up to now, Sir, what has he promised to do for you, exactly?

CALLIMACO. He's promised to persuade Lord Nicia to go with his wife to a mineral bath resort this coming May.

SIRO. But how will that help you, master? I really don't see—

CALLIMACO. How will it help me? Well, maybe the new environment will work a few changes in the girl's personality— I mean, in places like that there's nothing to do but have a good time, go to lots of parties, lie around all day— ; and I could go there myself—organize all sorts of festivities, spend a lot of money— get to know her, and get to know her husband—well, I don't know. How can I predict what might happen? My grandmother's aunt used to say "From things come things, and Time governs all."

SIRO. Well—er—why not? —eh, master?

CALLIMACO. Ligurio just left me this morning, in fact—he said he'd talk to Lord Nicia and then come right back and let me know what was happening.

SIRO. Why, but look over there! There they are—

CALLIMACO. All right now, you go home—

SIRO. All right— I'm going. (*Siro exits. Callimaco goes to one side. Nicia and Ligurio enter.*)

ACT ONE

SCENE 2

NICIA. That was a good suggestion, my boy—those baths— I brought it up with my wife last night, but you know she has to *think* about things. Heh! In a way I'm hoping we won't have to go.

LIGURIO. Oh—really?

NICIA. Well, I hate to leave my little nest, you know. And to have to take along a wife and a household—maids, clothing, dining utensils—it's not fun, my friend. And do you know what else? Last night I talked to a few of those doctors: one of them said I should go to San Filippo; and then the next one said no, I should go to Poretta; and then the next one said no, well Villa is by *far* the best. What idiots, really. I mean, these so-called doctors don't know what's nibbling at the end of their line, if you get my meaning.

LIGURIO. Ha ha— Well—yes— Yes I can imagine that the thought of a long journey—all that travelling! —must be displeasing to a man of the city like yourself— I mean, I know it must pain you to travel to places where you can't even see Il Duomo—aha ha—

NICIA. What? No—but that's just where you're wrong, my friend! Travel? Listen—when I was younger, good Lord, I used to wander just everywhere—if they held a fair in Prato, why, there I'd be; and there wasn't a single castle in the province that I hadn't visited. And I'll tell you something else: I've been to Pisa, and I've been to Livorno. So don't tell *me* that I don't like to travel. (*Pause.*)

LIGURIO. You must have seen the Leaning Tower of Pisa.

NICIA. I saw the Leaning Tower of Livorno, that's for sure.

LIGURIO. Oh—erp—yes, that's the one I meant. Oh yes, by the way, did you also see the sea at Livorno?

NICIA. Did I see the sea? You know very well that I saw it, my friend.

LIGURIO. Well how much bigger was it than the Arno, would you say?

NICIA. Bigger? Than the Arno? Well my dear fellow, it was surely four times as big— I mean, maybe even six or more times—when I say—and I mean—it was probably more like seven times bigger, one would almost say—and do you know the astonishing thing— I remember this so clearly—you just look out there, and all you can see is water—water—water—

LIGURIO. Yes— God—that's *so* true, isn't it? —But then you know I'm almost amazed, seeing as you seem to have—ha ha— "urinated in banks of snow like these," to coin a phrase, that you seem to find it so taxing just to think of going to one of these nearby mineral bath resorts—

NICIA. But—"you have a mouth full of milk," my dear fellow, if you'll excuse an old expression— I mean, you don't seem to know

17

much about life, my boy, you've remained a baby. Can't you see how different it is from a young man's wanderings, when you have responsibilities, a family—a domestic establishment that you have to somehow take apart and put back together again in some distant place? (*Pause.*) But it's true—my desire to have children makes my life a torment— I'll do anything in order to have children. You talk with those doctors, though, for me, would you? Find out where they think I ought to go. I'll talk with my wife and meet you later.

LIGURIO. Certainly, my Lord. Certainly—that's fine. (*Nicia exits.*)

ACT ONE

SCENE 3

LIGURIO. (*Alone.*) I'd be surprised if there's a stupider person in the world than this worthless man. And yet look how Fortune has favored him! He's disgustingly rich. His wife is ravishing; she's elegant; she's smart. She's clever enough to rule a kingdom, as a matter of fact; and instead, she's the wife of a fool. That's why I really hate that old proverb, "God makes men and women in a heap, and they sort themselves out into sweet little pairs." God— when I think how often I've seen really good men getting married to pigs, while the intelligent women give themselves willingly to maniacs and clowns . . . All the same, sometimes I get such exquisite pleasure out of listening to the man talk—it's just so perfect, I really enjoy it— (*Callimaco approaches.*) Ah! Callimaco!

CALLIMACO. What's happening, Ligurio? Tell me! Please!

LIGURIO. Well—you know Lord Nicia, my friend. He's a very pinched and petty little man, and he's afraid to leave the city. But I inspired him a bit. He ended up by saying that he'd do what I think best. So we could certainly get him to one of those resorts, if you still like that plan. But you know— I'm really no longer so certain that that plan would best serve our interests.

CALLIMACO. Really? But why?

LIGURIO. Well— I'm not quite sure. It's a feeling I have. You see, people of every kind come to these resorts. What if someone showed up there to whom this strikingly delicious-looking girl

18

seemed just as exciting as she does to you? —I mean someone let's say with a lot more money, or some devastating, irresistible charm— I mean, I don't know. But there's always that danger in a place like that—you wouldn't want to go to all that trouble just to benefit some other chap, if you see what I mean.

CALLIMACO. God— I know—that's absolutely right. But what can I do, then? What plan can I pursue? I mean, where can I turn? I mean— God! —don't you see— I've got to have a plan, I've got to *do something*—even if it's something insane, or dangerous, or even ruthless or evil! Because I would much rather die than go on living like this! If I could sleep at night, I mean if I could eat, if I could talk, if I could enjoy myself in any way at all, I'd be more patient, I could wait— I could wait for a more favorable moment; but there's no escape for me; there's no relief anywhere; and if I can't find immediately some plan to hang on to, I will certainly die in convulsions and frenzy; and when I realize that *this* may be the moment of my death, then I lose all my fears and hesitations, and I just can't wait to throw myself totally into the most bestial course of action! Yes, bestial! Bestial, cruel, and degraded! I'm ready— I'm ready—

LIGURIO. Please— Don't say such things— Can't you try to *control* your impetuosity?

CALLIMACO. You can see very well that precisely in order to control it I'm allowing my mind to range freely over all these various thoughts. In this way, you can see, I'm not doing any harm. But I mean it, I've got to have some hope to chew on— I don't care if it's even a false hope! —just anything to take this pressure off my brain—

LIGURIO. Yes, you're right, of course. And I'm right here with you, and I'm ready to do anything to help you out of your predicament.

CALLIMACO. I believe you. I mean— I know very well that people like you live only by deceiving other people. That's your whole way of life— I understand that very well. But I don't think it will cause me any trouble in this case, because you're very well aware that I'd become your enemy if I caught you trying to fool me—and then you'd lose the use of my very nice house, and you'd never get the money that I've promised to give you if my project goes well.

LIGURIO. Callimaco—please—please don't doubt me, Callimaco!

Even if this situation should turn out not to have in any way the financial benefit for me that I believe it will have and certainly hope it will have, nonetheless there still would be a reason to trust me, you see, because— I feel we're people of the same kind, the same blood, Callimaco. Yes, my blood flows together with yours, it really does, and my desire for you to achieve your chosen prize is, truly, almost as great as your own could ever be. —But let's not discuss this any more. The professor has asked me to find him a doctor, in order to determine which bath he ought to go to, and this provides us with a certain opportunity. But you must allow yourself to be guided by me. Believe me— I know what I'm doing. (*Pause.*) You must be that doctor. You only have to say that you've studied and practiced exclusively in Paris. The professor will certainly believe you if you behave like an educated man and manage to address him a few words in Latin.

CALLIMACO. But what purpose would this serve?

LIGURIO. Well—it *could* serve, of course, to send the old fellow to whatever bath we like. But it could also serve a certain other purpose. It could set us off on an entirely different path that I think I've discovered—a path that is shorter, less difficult, and more certain to lead to our goal than the path we've been considering.

CALLIMACO. What? Really? But what are you saying?

LIGURIO. I am saying that if you will be very bold, and trust entirely in me, I will have our business accomplished by this time tomorrow.

CALLIMACO. My heart is beginning to beat again. I can feel myself breathing. But how can you do it?

LIGURIO. I'll tell you when we have a free moment. There's no time to talk now—we'll hardly be able to do what needs to be done in the time that we have, much less have a long conversation. Please—go home quickly and wait for me there. I'll go find the professor. When I bring him to you, just follow my prompting and you'll know what I want you to say.

CALLIMACO. Of course—of course— I'll do it all, my dear friend, as you've filled me with a marvellous feeling that the future will be bright. Oh God, I feel hopeful—oh God—oh God—
(*Callimaco and Ligurio exit. Nymphs and shepherds enter and sing.*)

O Love, Love,
he who has never
tasted your strength
has no conception

20

of Heaven's greatest power.
Nor does he know
how
inside one breast
death and life can live side by side,
or how
under your awesome sway
a person may hide
from all that is good
and pursue the very thing
that most will harm him;
or how one can care for oneself
less than for another;
or how often and how quickly in succession
a human heart may be frozen
by fear
and thawed
by hope.
Nor can he know
how gods fear no less than men
the terrible arms with which you are armed.

ACT TWO

SCENE 1

(*Ligurio and Nicia.*)

LIGURIO. I'm telling you God has put this man on earth just for you, so that you can finally achieve your goal! The practice he had in Paris was truly remarkable. Your only problem is that he might not agree to take your case—he's so terribly busy. He's such a learned man!

NICIA. Really. Well, I shall discover for myself, after a few words of conversation, whether he knows anything or not; he won't sell *me* any bladders, as we say; when I buy a melon, I know how to squeeze the skin!

LIGURIO. Yes, by all means, test him out: see how he presents himself; listen to him speak; examine him carefully—

NICIA. But where does the man live, by the way?

LIGURIO. In this very same piazza, in that doorway there— (*He knocks on the door.*)

SIRO. (*From inside.*) Who is it?

LIGURIO. Is Callimaco at home?

SIRO. Yes. He is.

NICIA. But why don't you say "*Doctor* Callimaco?"

LIGURIO. He doesn't like these hollow formalities at all, my friend. (*Callimaco appears, dressed as a doctor.*)

ACT TWO

SCENE 2

CALLIMACO. Who is it who wants me?

NICIA. *Bona dies, domine magister.*

CALLIMACO. *Et vobis bona, domine doctor.*

LIGURIO. (*To Nicia.*) Well—what do you think?

NICIA. I say! —hm! —not bad—pretty good—really! —

LIGURIO. Heh heh—but now if you want the pleasure of *my*

company, old chaps, you'd better speak in a language I can understand—that Latin, you know—ha ha—well, otherwise we'll be like two different little families lighting their fires side by side, if you see what I mean.

CALLIMACO. What good things bring you here, gentlemen?

NICIA. How can I say this, Doctor: I'm looking for two things that another man might very well flee: in short, I want to cause trouble for myself, and trouble for the world. I don't have children, Doctor, and I want to have them, and in order to get for myself that special kind of trouble, I've come to bother you.

CALLIMACO. It could never be a bother to bring happiness, Sir, to you, or to men of real worth like yourself. I would not have exhausted myself studying for years in Paris if it was not so that I would some day be able to serve people just exactly like you.

NICIA. It's kind of you to say this; and believe me, if you ever have need of any *legal* assistance, Doctor, my goodness, I'd be happy to have the chance to help you out. —But now let's turn our thoughts to *rem nostram*— (*To Ligurio.*) *our business,* you see. (*To Callimaco.*) Have you considered which baths would be the best for preparing my wife for successful impregnation? I know that Ligurio has told you the details of the case—

CALLIMACO. Yes, he's told me a great deal. But if I'm to satisfy your desire, I must begin by discovering the specific cause of the sterility of your wife, because you must understand that there are of course many different possible causes of sterility: *nam causae sterilitatis sunt: aut in semine, aut in matrice, aut in strumentiis seminariis, aut in virga, aut in causa extrinseca.* (*To Ligurio.*) For the causes of sterility can lie in the uterus, or else in the semen, the testicles, or the shaft of the penis, or else in some extrinsic cause.

NICIA. This is the most extraordinary man I've ever met.

CALLIMACO. Aside from these causes, the failure of the wife to be fertilized can be caused by the impotence of the husband, and when this is the case there can of course be no cure for the sterility.

NICIA. Aha! Ha ha ha! Can you imagine *me* impotent? Aha ha ha ha! Yes, you will make me laugh, my dear Doctor! I am like a rod of iron, charged and pulsating with blood— I'm in my spring-time, my spring-time, Doctor—

CALLIMACO. If that is not the problem, you can be very optimistic that we will find some remedy. (*Aside.*) Heh, heh.

NICIA. Eh—what? —do you mean there might be some remedy other than the baths? Because you know I don't relish the difficulties of going to the baths, and my wife as well would leave Florence most unwillingly—

LIGURIO. Yes—there is another remedy— I will answer your question myself. Callimaco is too careful and cautious. (*To Callimaco*.) Well—haven't you told me that you know how to make certain potions that will infallibly cause pregnancy to occur?

CALLIMACO. Well—yes— I have—but I don't ordinarily mention this to people I don't know— I mean, I'd be afraid they might think I was some sort of a fraud, or a charlatan—ha ha—

NICIA. Doctor, I swear to you, with me you may put aside these fears entirely—entirely. I admire you—you have caused me to admire you so enormously that there isn't a thing I wouldn't believe from you, or a thing I wouldn't undertake to do, myself, under your supervision.

LIGURIO. (*To Callimaco*.) I believe you find it necessary to see the patient's urine—

CALLIMACO. Yes, that's the first step, of course.

LIGURIO. Call Siro, so that he can go with the professor to his house to obtain the sample and then bring it right back; we'll wait for it here, inside.

CALLIMACO. Siro! (*Siro appears*.) Siro, go with this gentleman. And, Professor, if you can spare a bit more time, perhaps it would be wise to come back here directly yourself, so we can make further plans.

NICIA. Good Lord—if I can spare a bit more time! Oh Doctor— I'll be back within one moment, I swear it. I have more faith in you than those little Hungarians have in their swords. Dear, good Doctor— (*Nicia and Siro move away from Callimaco and Ligurio. Callimaco and Ligurio go inside.*)

ACT TWO

SCENE 3

NICIA. (*To Siro*.) That master of yours is an extraordinary, remarkable man. A marvellous man.

SIRO. Yes—he certainly is.

NICIA. The King of France himself must know him and admire him.

24

SIRO. Yes, he admires him deeply.

NICIA. I suppose it's precisely for this reason that your master is so willing to remain there in France.

SIRO. Yes—that is the reason—yes—

NICIA. He does well to remain there. The people in this country are pieces of shit, if I may say so. They can't respect a man who has real ability. If your master had stayed here, he wouldn't have found a soul who would talk to him. I know what I'm saying. It's taken me hours and hours of straining and sweating in the library to come up with a few little turds of knowledge, my friend, if I may use a frank expression, but if I'd had to earn my living in this country from the knowledge I've amassed over years and years, I'd be freezing to death in the cold, I can tell you.

SIRO. But Sir—don't you make, at least, a hundred ducats a year?

NICIA. I don't make a hundred pennies! I don't make a hundred of those filthy little tokens! Let me tell you, my friend, if you don't have some very good connections to the people in power in this city— I mean, as a lawyer? —good Lord, there isn't even a dog who will bark in your face! (*Pause.*) But it doesn't bother me. I have plenty of money. I don't need clients . . . But all the same, I wouldn't want anyone to know I'd said these things—do you follow me, my boy? Those bastards would love to make me pay some special extra tax or cook up some other new boil on my ass to make me sweat, as we say.

SIRO. Er—don't worry about me, Sir—

NICIA. Well, this is my house. Just wait for me here; this won't take long.

SIRO. Whatever you like, Sir. (*Nicia goes in.*)

ACT TWO

SCENE 4

SIRO. You see, I'm just an uneducated man myself, and *he's* an educated man. And the people in my class are supposed to be dumber than the people in his class. But—if the educated class were made up of people like *him*—do you realize how dumb we'd have to be? We'd be spending all our days putting our dough into stone-cold ovens. And then we'd be wondering, why isn't it baking into bread? (*Pause.*) Obviously that evil Ligurio and that madman my master are leading this poor fool into some lonely corner, where they will perpetrate some shameful mischief on him. Well, I'm sure I'd find it amusing, if only I could believe that the story would never come out. Because if the story does come out, I'm afraid my life will be in danger, and so will my master's, and all of his possessions. (*Nicia appears, with urine in a glass urinal.*)

ACT TWO

Scene 5

NICIA. (*As if to Lucrezia.*) I've done everything, everything your way. I'm asking you only to do this one thing my way—just one thing, one thing! If I had thought I wouldn't have children, I would have taken a peasant girl for my wife instead of you. (*To Siro.*) Come over here now, Siro; just take this and come along. (*He gives Siro the urinal.*) The agony I had to go through to get that bitch just to give me a sample of her urine— And the incredible thing is, it isn't as if she didn't care about not having children; she worries about it even more than I do! It's just that when I want her to do something—anything, anything—well then there's really a story to tell—really some story—
SIRO. Be patient, Sir: you know that a woman will usually do what one wants her to do, if one can only manage somehow to put the matter in the right way—
NICIA. The right way, eh? I'm sick of that bitch! I'm fed up—get it? Now hurry, please, and tell your master and Ligurio I'm here.
SIRO. Yes— (*Ligurio and Callimaco appear, at some distance from Nicia and Siro.*)

ACT TWO

Scene 6

LIGURIO. (*To Callimaco.*) The professor will be easy to persuade; the difficult thing will be to persuade his wife. But even with her, there are certain techniques—

26

CALLIMACO. (*To Nicia.*) Well well! Do you have the urine?

NICIA. Siro has it, underneath his cloak.

CALLIMACO. Give it here. (*He takes the urinal.*) Oh! But this urine shows weakness of the kidneys!

NICIA. Why—yes—why it is rather cloudy, now gentlemen, isn't it—and she only just passed it a moment ago!

CALLIMACO. Well, don't be *too* surprised, Sir, after all. *Nam mulieris urinae sunt sempre maioris glossitiei et albedinis, et minoris pulchritudinis, quam virorum. Huius autem, inter caetera, causa est amplitudo canalium, mixtio eorum quae ex matrice exeunt cum urina.* (*To Ligurio.*) For the urine of women is always much less attractive than the urine of men. It is coarser and whiter. And the cause of this may be, on the one hand, the width of the female canals, and on the other, the mixture of fluids from these same canals which exit from the lips of the genitals along with the urine.

NICIA. By the sacred vagina of Saint Pucci, this man grows more refined and brilliant as we hold him in our hands! Look at how well he reasons about these things—

CALLIMACO. I'm concerned that the lady doesn't have a satisfactory covering on top of her at night— (*Aside.*) heh heh—and for this reason produces cloudy urine.

NICIA. Why, but no—she always has at least a good quilt on top of her—but you know, she stays on her knees on the floor for *four hours* saying her prayers before she comes to bed—she's so silly, she's careless about the cold— (*Pause.*)

CALLIMACO. Well, in any case, Professor, here's the situation. Either you have faith in me, or not. Either I'm going to give you an infallible remedy for your problem, or I'm not. But if you do in fact take my remedy, and if a year from today your wife doesn't have a little child nestling in her arms—well—I promise you—I'll give you two thousand ducats.

NICIA. Then tell me your remedy, as I believe in you more than I believe in my confessor.

CALLIMACO. Fine. (*Pause.*) Then you must understand this— that there is no more certain way to make a woman pregnant than to cause her to drink a potion made from the root of the mandrake. This is something I've tested and tested again on countless occasions and always found to be true; and if it had not been true, then the Queen of France would be sterile today, and countless other princesses of that great state.

NICIA. What? —Is this possible? —

CALLIMACO. It is, Sir, just as I have said. And Fortune apparently loves you so well that I was able to bring with me from France all of the ingredients that go towards the making of this potion—and you may have this potent beverage at your own convenience.

NICIA. But when do you recommend that my wife should take the potion, Doctor?

CALLIMACO. Well—this evening after supper. The moon is well disposed, and the time could not be more appropriate.

NICIA. My goodness! All right then—this won't be a problem. Prepare the potion, by all means, and I will make my wife drink it.

CALLIMACO. Good. (*Pause.*) It's also necessary to mention one more point, I would say: it happens to be true that the first man to have intercourse with the woman after she's taken this potion will die within eight days, and nothing in the world can save him.

NICIA. Bloody shit! Is this the vinegar in your sugary little drink? Well then I won't have any—thank you! You're not going to hang me with *that* rope, my friends! Oh really, really—you've really destroyed me— I'm so upset—

CALLIMACO. Get ahold of yourself. There's a solution to this problem.

NICIA. Really. What is it?

CALLIMACO. The solution is to cause another man, whom you have chosen, to have intercourse with your wife immediately after she's taken this potion; staying with her for one night, he will absorb all the infection of the mandrake; and as soon as he's left, you can fuck her yourself without the slightest concern.

NICIA. Well, I don't want to use that solution, my friend.

CALLIMACO. Why not, Professor?

NICIA. Because I don't want to make my wife into a prostitute—frankly. And I don't want to be the cause of my own betrayal, Sir, if you really want to know.

CALLIMACO. But what are you saying, Professor? Really, you don't seem to be as sensible as I originally took you to be. Do you really mean that you hesitate to do a thing that the King of France, and many of the greatest lords of that state, have not hesitated to do?

NICIA. But my dear Doctor, who do you want me to find to carry out this madness—eh? If I tell the man, then he won't want to do

28

it. And if I don't tell him, I would be leading him to his death by means of a trick— I think I would have a legal problem there, now don't you, Doctor? I don't think I *want* that sort of problem—not at all, my friend—

CALLIMACO. Listen to me—if it's only this that bothers you, leave the matter in my hands, and I'll take care of it myself.

NICIA. But what will you do, Sir?

CALLIMACO. I'll tell you. (*Pause.*) This evening, after supper, I will give you the potion; you will give it to your wife to drink and get her as quickly as possible into her bed; this should be around —ten o'clock. —Then we'll all disguise ourselves—you, Ligurio, Siro, and I—and we'll go down through the New Market and the Old Market, and we'll look in every odd corner and walk down every tiny lane, and the first young moron we find wandering pointlessly through the streets or lounging around in some shadowy gutter—well, we'll gag him, we'll knock him on the head with some small baton or club, and we'll convey him to your house, put him in your bed, and tell him what to do. Then, in the morning, you can throw the boy out, give your wife a good wash, and enjoy her yourself without a care in the world. (*Long silence.*)

NICIA. Well—all right—I'll go along with your plan—since you say that the King and princes and lords have used this same method. But it's of the utmost importance that the matter be kept absolutely secret—for legal reasons, for *legal* reasons . . .

CALLIMACO. Who do you think would mention it?

NICIA. And there's still one problem, and it's a serious one, my friends.

CALLIMACO. And what is that?

NICIA. The problem of getting my wife to go along with this plan, which I believe she will never in the least be disposed to do.

CALLIMACO. I'm sure you're right. But I shouldn't like to be married in the first place if I couldn't compel my wife to do what I was disposed to *having* her do.

LIGURIO. I've thought of the solution to this problem.

NICIA. You what?

LIGURIO. We can arrange the matter through the friar—her confessor.

CALLIMACO. Oh—but who will arrange the confessor—you?

LIGURIO. Yes—I will; and so will you; and so will a bit of money, along with our own undoubted shrewdness, and the well-known shrewdness of all confessors.

NICIA. I'm doubtful, though, whether on my recommendation my wife would even be willing to talk to her confessor.

LIGURIO. There is also a solution to this.

NICIA. My dear fellow—

LIGURIO. She can at least be brought to talk to her mother—

NICIA. Yes—she trusts her mother—

LIGURIO. And I know that her mother will be of our opinion; she's an old friend of mine, you know, dear Madonna Sostrata . . . (*To Callimaco.*) Doctor, I shall see you here at seven! (*Ligurio and Nicia begin to move off. Callimaco addresses Ligurio, out of Nicia's hearing.*)

CALLIMACO. But wait—no—don't leave me alone—please—

LIGURIO. You seem to be somehow drunk, Doctor—

CALLIMACO. But where do you want me to go *right now?*

LIGURIO. Well take a walk, Doctor— I mean, go to the cathedral, go to that rotting old fortress by the lake— I mean, this is *Florence*, old Doctor, one of the world's great cities! —

CALLIMACO. No—no—don't leave me—I'm dying— (*Nicia, Ligurio, and Callimaco exit. Nymphs and shepherds enter and sing.*)

How happy would
anyone be
if he could see
this person who is born a fool
and believes
anything.
Blind to reality,
opportunities
don't
entice him,
fear
doesn't
torment him—
he escapes these seeds
of anxiety and pain.
The man longs
to have children
and to feed his hopes
would believe that

30

horses
fly.
How sad! How sad!
He's cast all other wishes
into darkness
and on that one hope only
has fixed all his desire.

ACT THREE

SCENE 1

(Ligurio, Nicia, and Sostrata.)

SOSTRATA. Well, they say that clever people can choose the better of bad alternatives—isn't that right? If you want to have children, and you don't have a means that's better than this one, well then, you'd better use this one, my boy—that's to say, so long as it's no trouble to your conscience, Son.

NICIA. That's right, Mother.

LIGURIO. Then you must talk to your daughter, Madonna, while Lord Nicia and I will be finding the friar, Brother Timothy, and telling him our story.

SOSTRATA. Good. That road over there is the road to the church. I'll take the road over to your house, Son, and I'll convince my girl somehow to talk to her confessor.

LIGURIO. Very good. That's fine. *(Sostrata exits.)*

ACT THREE

SCENE 2

LIGURIO. Well now, my Lord, I think you'd better give me twenty-five ducats—if you can spare it, that is. You know, it's sometimes best in this sort of situation—dealing with religious folk, I mean—to spend a bit of money and become a friend of the person right away, and then give him hope for something better.

NICIA. Go ahead, take it. It doesn't bother me a bit; I'll make it up somewhere else, my friend.

LIGURIO. Now you see—these monks, these friars—they're extremely sophisticated—very subtle and deep in their dealings; and you can see why they would be, because they know all of our sins —as well as their own; in other words, I mean, if you're not very familiar with them, you can get nothing from them; in fact, they'll

32

destroy you. So, you see, I wouldn't want you to make any mistakes and unintentionally harm our interests in our conversation with the friar—because someone like you—you spend all your days in the library, and you have a marvellous understanding of literature and books—but you may not know how to talk about the ordinary things of the work-a-day world. (*Aside.*) The things he might say—it could really be fatal—

NICIA. Well—tell me what you want me to do.

LIGURIO. Well—how long has it been since you last met the friar?

NICIA. It's been ten years at least—

LIGURIO. That's good. That's good. I'm going to tell him that you're deaf these days. Don't respond in any way, and don't say a word unless we speak very loudly.

NICIA. Heh heh—well—all right—I'll do it—

LIGURIO. Oh, and by the way, don't be upset if I need to say certain things that would seem on the outside to be—er—unhelpful, in relation to what we're trying to accomplish; it will all turn out to our purpose in the end.

NICIA. Yes— I get it— I follow you—that's fine, my friend—

LIGURIO. But I see the friar conversing with a woman over there. Let's wait here until he leaves her . . . (*Brother Timothy and a woman enter. Ligurio and Nicia stand at a distance.*)

ACT THREE

SCENE 3

BROTHER TIMOTHY. If you would like to confess, Madonna, I am ready to listen.

WOMAN. No, not today—people are waiting for me at home—it's enough for me just to unburden myself a little bit like this, just standing right here. (*Pause.*) Well— Did you say those Masses of Our Lady?

BROTHER TIMOTHY. Why yes—yes— I certainly did—

WOMAN. Then take this money, and for two months every Monday say the Mass of the Dead for my poor husband. Although he was coarse and rough—a swine, really—he thrilled me as a man. The flesh is so powerful— I can't help feeling something even now

33

when I think of him; would you believe it? (*Pause.*) But do you think he's in Purgatory now, truly, Father?

BROTHER TIMOTHY. Without a doubt.

WOMAN. Well— I'm still not sure of it . . . You know what he did to me a few times . . . Oh, Father, how often I came to talk to you about him, to complain— I avoided him whenever I could— but he never got tired—he just kept after me, after me—oh Father —oh Lord—

BROTHER TIMOTHY. Don't worry, my child, God's mercy is great: if man doesn't lack the will to repent, he will never lack the opportunity. (*Pause.*)

WOMAN. Do you think the Turks will arrive in Italy this year?

BROTHER TIMOTHY. If you don't say your prayers, I'm afraid so, yes.

WOMAN. Oh no! God help us! God help us, we'll be trapped by those murderers, those fiends— I have such terrible fears of being impaled by a Turk! —Oh—but that woman over there in the church has some linen of mine. I'd better go find her. Have a good day, Father.

BROTHER TIMOTHY. Go in good health. (*The woman exits. Ligurio and Nicia remain at a distance from Brother Timothy, and he doesn't see them.*)

ACT THREE

SCENE 4

BROTHER TIMOTHY. Yes. You see, women are much more favorably disposed towards charity than men. They give much more freely. But it can be a kind of torture to talk with them— sometimes, they're so boring—even, almost sickening . . . — If you drive them all away, you can avoid a lot of grueling conversation, but you lose a lot of money. —If you encourage their visits, you can find yourself exhausted and depressed, but it's very rewarding. Well, they always say, "No honey without flies!" A noble old saying— (*Ligurio and Nicia approach, and he addresses them.*) Oh! But what are you up to, good gentlemen? Do I not recognize the distinguished Lord Nicia?

34

LIGURIO. Speak loudly! —he's grown so deaf that he can't hear a thing any more.

BROTHER TIMOTHY. It's so pleasant to see you both here, good Sirs.

LIGURIO. Louder—

BROTHER TIMOTHY. —to see you here—

NICIA. —to find *you*, Father!

BROTHER TIMOTHY. Yes! . . . But what *are* you fine gentlemen up to these days— ? —eh? —

NICIA —everything's *fine*—

LIGURIO. Father, I think you'd better address your remarks just to me; I mean, in order to make *him* understand, you'd have to set the entire *piazza* resounding with your voice—aha ha ha—

BROTHER TIMOTHY. Well, what do you want of me, boys?

LIGURIO. This distinguished Professor Nicia, Father, and another good man, whom you will hear about later, have a few hundred ducats to spend on charity—

NICIA. Bloody shit!

LIGURIO. Don't be surprised, Father, at the things he says; he can't hear, but you know sometimes he *thinks* that he hears things, and he responds to *these* and of course well you know this is *inappropriate*—heh heh heh—

BROTHER TIMOTHY. Yes, just keep talking, and we'll let him say what he likes.

LIGURIO. Yes. Well, I have a part of the money with me, and these men want *you* to distribute it, Father.

BROTHER TIMOTHY. Well! Fine!

LIGURIO. But it happens to be necessary, before these alms can be distributed, that you give us some help in an odd situation that's come up for this gentleman, and it turns out, strangely, that you're the *only* person who can help us in this case, and it's actually a situation in which the entire honor of the gentleman's house is at stake.

BROTHER TIMOTHY. Really. What situation is this, actually?

LIGURIO. Now I'm not sure you know Camillo Calfucci, the nephew of this gentleman.

BROTHER TIMOTHY. Yes, I know him.

LIGURIO. Well, Calfucci, you see, went to France a year ago in connection with certain business ventures of his, and not having a wife—she had died, unfortunately—he left a rather young daughter of his in the care of a convent, whose name there's no need to mention for the moment—

BROTHER TIMOTHY. And the consequence of this—

LIGURIO. The consequence, unfortunately—whether we should blame the negligence of the nuns or the childish little brain of the poor girl herself—the consequence is that she finds herself four months pregnant, Father, with the result that if the situation isn't skillfully handled—well—the professor here, the nuns, the child, and Camillo will all be subject to the most terrible disgrace; and the professor here considers the danger of this disgrace so grave a matter that he's vowed that if the case is laid to rest successfully he will give three hundred ducats for the love of God.

NICIA. The most incredible nonsense! —

LIGURIO. And he'll give the money right into *your* hands; and you and the abbess are the only two people in the world who can help us . . .

BROTHER TIMOTHY. What would you want me to do?

LIGURIO. Well—persuade the abbess to give the child a potion that would cause her to miscarry.

BROTHER TIMOTHY. This is really something to think about.

LIGURIO. Well what do you mean, something to think about? Look, don't you see all the good things that would come out of this? Come on, Father! You'd be preserving the honor of this convent! And also of this little child, and all of her relatives! You would really be giving a daughter back to her father, and you would be bringing great relief of mind to this distinguished gentleman here and to so many members of his family. And you could help a lot of people with those three hundred ducats. And for God's sake, you wouldn't be *harming* anyone if you did this thing for us —except a piece of meat not yet born, without the ability to feel sensations, that might well be aborted in any event in any number of different possible ways. And as far as the moral implications of this matter are concerned, *I've* always thought—pardon me if I'm wrong—that "goodness" means whatever is helpful to the most people, and pleases the most people the most—do you agree with me, Father?

BROTHER TIMOTHY. Oh yes. Oh certainly. Yes, it must be done, in the name of God. Let it be done. For God's sake and charity's sake, may every thing be done. It shall be accomplished, just as you wish it. Tell me the name of the convent. Give me the potion. And, if you think it's right, you can give me a portion of the money right away, so I can begin to do a few worthy things . . .

LIGURIO. Now you're acting like the sort of monk I believed you to be. Take this part of the money. The convent is— But wait a moment—that woman over there—inside the church— I think she's beckoning to me; I think I'd better go see what she wants. I'll be back in a moment; don't leave Professor Nicia, Father; I think I'd better talk with this person. (*Ligurio exits. Silence.*)

ACT THREE

SCENE 5

BROTHER TIMOTHY. How old is this poor child we've been talking about? —

NICIA. —it's *really* incredible—

BROTHER TIMOTHY. I say, how old is that poor child?

NICIA. May God curse and ruin him!

BROTHER TIMOTHY. Heh heh—but why? —

NICIA. Because he deserves it!

BROTHER TIMOTHY. (*Aside.*) Obviously I've fallen into a dangerous swamp. Yes—it's definitely slippery and creepy. Handicapped people. A deaf person. A mad person. The mad one's run off. And the deaf one can't understand what I'm saying. Well— why not? Unless this is counterfeit money, and it's not, I can still come out of this healthy, though dealing with the sick. (*Ligurio enters.*)

ACT THREE

SCENE 6

LIGURIO. Oh, I've got wonderful news, Father!

BROTHER TIMOTHY. Really?

LIGURIO. That woman, with whom I've just spoken—she just told me that the child has miscarried all by herself! Now isn't that great?

BROTHER TIMOTHY. Well! My my! These alms will go into the municipal treasury.

LIGURIO. But what are you saying?

BROTHER TIMOTHY. I was saying that now you have more reason than ever to give these alms to the poor.

LIGURIO. Well of course the alms will be given—whenever you like, Father; but it's still necessary for you to do a certain *other* thing for the benefit of this gentleman here, you see, actually.

BROTHER TIMOTHY. A certain— ? —

LIGURIO. Something much less alarming—much less likely to incur blame or scandal—but still something even more welcome to us, and it will be even more helpful for you, as well.

BROTHER TIMOTHY. Oh—do tell me. You see, I'm really *allied* with you now; I feel really that there's such an intimacy that has grown up between us that there really isn't anything I wouldn't do for you.

LIGURIO. Yes, but you know, I'd like to go inside the church, just to discuss this between the two of us, actually. The professsor will be happy to wait for us here . . . (*To Nicia.*) We'll be back in a moment!

NICIA. "I can't wait for you to return!" — (*Aside.*) —as the wounded toad said to the plough that left him bleeding . . . (*Ligurio and Brother Timothy exit.*)

ACT THREE

Scene 7

NICIA. Is this day, or night? Am I awake? Am I dreaming? I can't remember—am I drunk? —but I've had nothing to drink yet today—and yet I'm standing here, listening to these ravings, these absurdities . . . —We came here to tell the friar one thing—and he told him—he told him—and then he wanted me to pretend to be deaf, and really I ought to have smothered my ears the way Uggeri the Dane and his horse did when they wanted to shield themselves from the cries of Bravieri who was actually in league with demons, and—no, the things they were saying, the insanities, and to God knows what purpose! I've lost twenty-five ducats already, and he still hasn't said a word about my problem; and now they have me waiting here, suspended in the air like one of those limp little rolls that are stuck on those ugly long pins— But here they are coming back; and they're going to find themselves in very bad trouble if they haven't yet discussed my problem, I mean it . . . (*Ligurio and Brother Timothy return and approach Nicia.*)

ACT THREE

SCENE 8

BROTHER TIMOTHY. Arrange for the ladies to come and see me. I know what to do. And if my authority has any weight, the coupling we hope for will be accomplished this evening.

LIGURIO. Lord Nicia, Brother Timothy is ready now to do all that is necessary. I'm just going to step over and alert Madonna Sostrata, so she can bring your wife right over here directly. Then I'll return and meet you, inside the church.

NICIA. You rejuvenate me more than I can say. Will the child be male?

LIGURIO. A male child. (*He exits.*)

NICIA. I'm weeping with tenderness and gratitude—

BROTHER TIMOTHY. (*To Nicia.*) You may go into the church, and I'll wait right here for the ladies. But you must stand way over there, so that they won't be able to see you; and then when they've left, I'll tell you everything they said. (*Nicia exits.*)

ACT THREE

SCENE 9

BROTHER TIMOTHY. People are being manipulated here. People are being shamelessly used. But it's strange— I can't tell who is using whom. (*Pause.*) Obviously that villain Ligurio told me that first story only in order to test my reaction; if I once agreed to help him in that case, which was imaginary of course, he knew he could easily obtain my consent to help him in this one, which is real; if I had refused my help in the imaginary case, he would never have mentioned the real one, because they didn't want to disclose their design unless they had to, whereas it cost them nothing to tell me a made-up story which could never have gotten them into trouble. It's true— I was fooled by this device; but the trick redounds to my benefit. Lord Nicia and Callimaco are both very rich; I stand to gain a great deal from both of them, and, for their very different reasons, both of them are going to allow me to do so. And best of all, it's highly unlikely that the story will ever be known, because it's just as important for them to keep it quiet as it is for me. (*Pause.*) Well—whatever happens, I won't repent of it. (*Pause.*) One thing is certain: I don't think it's going to be easy to accomplish the matter, because the girl is actually such a good person; but I'm going to approach her precisely through her goodness. And when you get right down to it, no woman is ever really intelligent; they can all be fooled. Of course, if a woman speaks nicely and knows how to string a few sentences together, everyone praises her intelligence; but that's just like praising the intelligence of a little pig that's been taught to play a tune on one of those cute little horns; I mean—well—a pig that can do *that*—is an intelligent pig . . . But here she comes now, and there's her mother too—a real animal, if there ever was one; she'll be helpful, I think, in convincing her daughter to submit to my opinion and will— (*Sostrata and Lucrezia enter. At first they converse together at some distance from Brother Timothy.*)

ACT THREE

SCENE 10

SOSTRATA. My dear little girl— I know you believe me when I tell you that I value your honor and your welfare as much as anyone could in the world, and I would never advise you to do something that wasn't in your very best interest. I've told you, and I'll tell you again, that if Brother Timothy says such a thing should not be a burden to your conscience, then you may do it, my dear, without brooding any longer about it.

LUCREZIA. I have always worried that Lord Nicia's desire to have children might some day lead us both into some sort of terrible error; and for that very reason, whenever he has spoken to me on the subject of children, I have listened with apprehension, and even

40

suspicion. But of all the things that have been attempted in order to end our childless condition, this one seems to me surely the most strange—to submit my body to an act of vile humiliation, which in its turn will be the cause of another person's death—
SOSTRATA. There are so many things I don't know how to tell you, my darling. Please—talk to the friar, see what he says, and then do what he advises, what we advise you, dear, what everyone who loves you advises—
LUCREZIA. I am sweating from emotion, from passion— (*They approach Brother Timothy.*)

ACT THREE

SCENE 11

BROTHER TIMOTHY. Ladies, you are very welcome here. I know what you have come to ask me about, as Lord Nicia has told me all the details. And in fact I've been poring over my books for more than two hours doing research on this question; and after scrutinizing the literature very carefully, I have found many things that, both in general and in detail, accord remarkably well with the very course of action that we're now considering.
LUCREZIA. Are you speaking seriously, Father? —or perhaps you're joking? —
BROTHER TIMOTHY. Ah, Madonna Lucrezia! Would I joke about matters such as these? Don't you know me better than that?
LUCREZIA. Father, I do; but this seems to me the strangest thing that ever was heard of. —
BROTHER TIMOTHY. Madonna, I do believe you, but I don't want to hear you talking in this way any more, because I want you to listen to me. (*Pause.*) My child— (*Pause.*) —there are things in this world that we see at first from a distance, and we don't know much about them, and we think they must be very strange indeed—strange, un-natural—maybe even vile, sickening, demonic, evil. But then later we approach a bit closer to these very same things; we get to know more about them; and suddenly—why, they no longer seem so strange; we realize that they're really quite natural, quite normal, quite familiar, quite human, and even quite ordinary. And so we say about these things that they frighten us

41

out of all proportion to the danger that lies within them. And this thing we are discussing is one of these things.

LUCREZIA. May God so will it.

BROTHER TIMOTHY. But let me tell you some of the thoughts that came to me during those hours I spent sitting in my library. (*Pause.*) You see, in matters of conscience, of ethics, there is one principle whose logic you must always and invariably follow. This is the principle that when, in some given circumstance, an *uncertain* evil must be balanced against a *certain* good, then you must never forego that good out of fear of that evil. Now here in this case we have a certain good, namely that you would become pregnant, that you would obtain a soul for God's blessed harvest. The uncertain evil is that the man who lies with you after you take this potion will possibly die—because it has been found that there are some who *don't* die, of course; though, because the outcome is doubtful, it would still be unwise for Lord Nicia to run that risk. (*Pause.*) As for the act itself—the possibility that the act itself might be sinful—this is a children's fairy-tale, because it is the *will* that sins, and not the body; and the reason for sin would be the dis-pleasing of your husband—but in this case you would actually be pleasing him—or, on the other hand, the pleasure that you yourself might take in the act, but in this case it will cause you only displeasure. Finally, apart from these considerations, you must never forget that the *purpose,* the ultimate end of the possible action, is the chief thing to consider in all moral questions of any kind at all. Your purpose here is to fill a seat in paradise and content your husband, and it is that good purpose which you must realize to be of over-riding importance in this particular case. Indeed, the Bible tells us that the daughters of Lot, believing themselves to be the only women left in the world, actually used their own father for sexual intercouse; but because their purpose was good, they did not sin.

LUCREZIA. What are you trying to persuade me to do, Father?

SOSTRATA. Let yourself be persuaded, my darling. Don't you see that a woman who has no children has no home in the world? When her husband dies, she is left alone like an animal, abandoned —no one will help her! —

BROTHER TIMOTHY. I swear to you, Madonna, by this consecrated bosom, that there is as much to unsettle your conscience in the action of obeying your husband with deference in this matter as there is in eating meat on a Wednesday during the season of Advent, which is a sin that is washed away with a few tiny drops of holy water . . .

LUCREZIA. Where are you leading me, Father?

BROTHER TIMOTHY. I'm leading you to things for which you will always have reason to offer prayers to God for the benefit of my soul; and I can only say to you, you may not be happy about this now, but you'll be happy about it a year from today.

SOSTRATA. She will do it, Father; she will do the thing you want her to do. I'll tuck her into her little bed myself tonight—yes I will. Oh, what are you afraid of, my dear little mucus-nose? There are so many women in this city who would raise their hands to the sky in thanks to God if only they could be given a chance like yours. (Pause.)

LUCREZIA. Please. Please. I'll do—the thing. (Pause.) But I don't believe I ever will see tomorrow's morning.

BROTHER TIMOTHY. Don't worry, my daughter: I will pray to God for you, I will say the prayer of the Angel Rafael, that he may guide you, as he guided Tobias when Tobias trod on trembling foot into the doomed bedchamber of Sara, holding in his hand the great fish's entrails— Go now, and prepare yourself for this mystery, as it is already evening.

SOSTRATA. Be well, Father.

LUCREZIA. May God help me. May the blessed Virgin Mary, Mother of God, save me and protect me from sin and death. (Lucrezia and Sostrata exit.)

ACT THREE

SCENE 12

BROTHER TIMOTHY. Oh Ligurio, come out! (Ligurio and Nicia enter.)

LIGURIO. How did it go?

BROTHER TIMOTHY. Very well, very well. They're on their way home now to get everything ready, and I think all will go smoothly.

NICIA. Is this really true?

43

BROTHER TIMOTHY. Say—that's wonderful—are you cured of your deafness?

LIGURIO. Saint Clement has had mercy on my friend.

BROTHER TIMOTHY. Ah—you should put up a votive image of your ear in my church, my Lord, on Saint Clement's altar.

NICIA. I'm the happiest man in the entire world.

BROTHER TIMOTHY. Yes, I believe it.

LIGURIO. But go now, Brother, go to your prayers. And you, my Lord, go to your wife and hold her firm in her decision. I will find Doctor Callimaco, and we'll all meet together on the corner at ten, in our disguises.

BROTHER TIMOTHY. Yes. Good. Go in good health. (*All exit. Nymphs and shepherds enter and sing.*)

> So lovely this deception
> that leads to this end so dearly imagined
> and so dear,
> that takes away suffering
> and discards it
> like a cloak
> tossed in a corner,
> and makes every bitter taste
> sweet.
> Oh sublime, rare Crookedness—
> you show a straight road
> to wandering souls,
> and by making them happy
> you marvellously make Love rich.
> O wondrous Deception,
> you conquer
> with your cleverness alone
> stones
> poisons
> and enchantments.

(Pause.)

ACT FOUR

Scene 1

(*Callimaco enters.*)

CALLIMACO. I must say, I wish I knew what those fellows were up to. Is it possible I'll never see my friend Ligurio again? He said seven o'clock—but now it's eight! Oh God, the anxiety—the anxiety— I'm like a little boat, blown about the sea . . . (*Pause.*) Often I try to get control over myself, and I say to myself: What are you doing? Are you insane? When you finally get her, what will it come to? At that very instant, you'll finally understand your mistake and repent of all the struggles and torments you've endured for the sake of that pitiful moment. Don't you know how little good is actually found in the things that man desires, compared with what he assumes he will find? God! God! — But then I say to myself: Are you really such a coward? Can't you look into the face of your fate? Can't you fight for what you want? —And I fortify my heart and my morale and shore up my strength for the battle. But I don't remain strong for very long, because soon once again I am overwhelmed by such a pulsating desire to make love to that unspeakably beautiful woman just once, just once, that I can feel my entire body bubbling and broiling. And then I can't speak; my eyes seem to be dazzled, as if by the sun; and my brain seems to spin about dizzily inside my head at an incredible speed. (*Pause.*) At least, if I could have found Ligurio, I could have expressed these feelings to someone. (*Ligurio enters. At first he is at a distance from Callimaco and doesn't see him.*)

ACT FOUR

Scene 2

LIGURIO. Where in the world can he be? I've been to the *Piazza*, the Market, the Bench of the Spini, and the Gallery of the Torna-quinci, and now I'm back at his house. He must be wandering fast.

People in love have quicksilver under their feet and can't stop
moving.
CALLIMACO. Ligurio!
LIGURIO. Callimaco—
CALLIMACO. What's the news?
LIGURIO. Good news.
CALLIMACO. Actually good?
LIGURIO. The best.
CALLIMACO. You mean she'll do it?
LIGURIO. She will.
CALLIMACO. The friar really did what he was supposed to?
LIGURIO. Yes. He did it.
CALLIMACO. Oh holy friar! Oh Ligurio— I shall always implore
God on my knees to help this fine monk in all his endeavors!
LIGURIO. Well—the friar may need something more than your
prayers. —
CALLIMACO. Well of course—
LIGURIO. Well I mean—
CALLIMACO. Well, how much have you promised him?
LIGURIO. Three hundred ducats.
CALLIMACO. Oh—well, that's really not bad. And did you see
the mother too?
LIGURIO. We certainly did. And when she learned that her
daughter could have an evening of wonderful, innocent joy without
the danger of sin, she couldn't have been more eager to help us.
CALLIMACO. Oh, how nice—how nice it all is! —Dear God, for
what merit of mine have I deserved such good results as these?
LIGURIO. Do you have the potion ready?
CALLIMACO. Yes, I have it.
LIGURIO. What are you planning to send them, by the way?
CALLIMACO. Oh, it's just a nice liqueur, made with wine and
some spices, some cinnamon, some sugar— ; some people say it
even has an aphrodisiac aspect— (Pause.) Oh! Oh God—oh no!
Oh God! God! Oh no! This is terrible, terrible! Oh God! I'm
destroyed!
LIGURIO. What? What's wrong? You —
CALLIMACO. There's no solution—oh no—
LIGURIO. But what—are—what? —
CALLIMACO. It's all for nothing. I've walled myself up in the
oven. I can't get out of it—

46

LIGURIO. What do you mean? Can't you speak? Please—take your hands away from your face—please—please—

CALLIMACO. Oh God—don't you realize, I told the professor that you and he and Siro and I would go find someone to put in the bed with his wife? —

LIGURIO. Yes—yes—

CALLIMACO. What do you mean, yes—yes? Don't you get it? If I am with you looking for the boy, I won't be the one who gets picked to be put in the bed. But if I'm not with you, he's bound to figure out the whole scheme.

LIGURIO. Well yes—that's true. But isn't there a solution for this problem?

CALLIMACO. Well I really don't think that there is.

LIGURIO. Well, there certainly must be.

CALLIMACO. Well what is it, then?

LIGURIO. Well I'd just like to think it over briefly.

CALLIMACO. Oh well thanks. Thanks a lot. That makes it pretty clear. I'm really destroyed, if you have to think now.

LIGURIO. I've got the solution.

CALLIMACO. Really? What is it?

LIGURIO. The friar has helped us so far. I'm going to ask him to help us again.

CALLIMACO. But how can he help?

LIGURIO. We're all going to be in disguise—right? I'll have him disguise himself also; he'll imitate your voice and your appearance, your style of dress; and I'll tell the professor it's you; and the professor will believe it.

CALLIMACO. Yes— I like that. But what will I do?

LIGURIO. Well—you should put on some raggedy short cloak and just come out from over there, from that corner by his house, with a lute in your hand, singing a little song.

CALLIMACO. With an uncovered face?

LIGURIO. Yes, because if you wear a mask, then he really would become suspicious.

CALLIMACO. But he'll recognize me.

LIGURIO. No, he won't, because I want you to distort your face; you see, you can open your mouth and sort of gnash your teeth, keep one eye closed— Here, try it a bit.

CALLIMACO. Is this all right?

LIGURIO. No—not really—

CALLIMACO. Like this? —

LIGURIO. Even more—

CALLIMACO. This? —

LIGURIO. Yes—yes—remember that position. I also have a good *fake nose* at home; I want you to wear that too.

CALLIMACO. Well then—what will happen next?

LIGURIO. Well, as you appear around the corner, we'll be waiting for you, and we'll snatch away your lute, and seize you roughly, and turn you around a bit so you won't know where you're going or what's happening, and then we'll take you to the house and put you in the bed. The rest you'll have to do for yourself.

CALLIMACO. Don't worry about the rest; your job, my friend, is just to get me in the house.

LIGURIO. That's right. Exactly. And tonight I'll get you into it. But if you want to be able to return, my friend—that you must arrange for yourself; with that I can't help you.

CALLIMACO. But what do you mean, though?

LIGURIO. I mean from now on the girl herself must become your accomplice, and you must win her to your side within the course of this night. Before you leave her, you must tell her who you are; you must reveal the trick; you must convey to her the deep, enduring passion that you feel, and explain that without any danger of disgrace she can become your lover—though if she chooses to be your enemy, her disgrace could be very great indeed. It's impossible that she won't be won over by you, and impossible that she would want this night to be the only such night.

CALLIMACO. Do you really believe this?

LIGURIO. Yes. I'm sure of it— But let's not lose time—it's already past eight. —Call Siro—send the potion to Lord Nicia's— I will go to Brother Timothy, put him in disguise and bring him here, and then we'll meet the professor and accomplish all that's left to be accomplished.

CALLIMACO. Very good. Go ahead. (*Ligurio exits.*)

ACT FOUR

Scene 3

CALLIMACO. Siro— (*Siro enters.*)

SIRO. My master—

CALLIMACO. I want you to find the silver goblet that's in my bedroom closet; cover it with a bit of cloth, bring it here, and be careful that you don't spill any of the contents on the way.

SIRO. Right. (*Siro exits.*)

CALLIMACO. This man has been with me for ten long years and has always served me faithfully. You know, I haven't told him what's happening—but I'm sure he's guessed it; you see, he's very shrewd! —he has a sort of a *criminal mind*, I'd almost say; and I can just see him adjusting to this present business—very happily . . . — (*Siro enters, with the goblet.*) Now hurry up, go quickly to Lord Nicia's, and tell him that this is the medicine his wife must take after supper.

SIRO. Right. (*Siro exits.*)

ACT FOUR

SCENE 4

CALLIMACO. If something wrecks this plan, tonight will be the very last night of my life. I shall throw myself into the Arno, or else hang myself, or else hurl myself out of one of those great big windows over there, or else stab myself to death in her very own doorway. (*Ligurio and Brother Timothy enter, at a distance from Callimaco. Brother Timothy is in disguise. Siro approaches them.*)

ACT FOUR

SCENE 5

SIRO. (*To Ligurio.*) Who's with you, Sir?

LIGURIO. A very great man.

SIRO. My—is he really *lame*? Or just pretending—

LIGURIO. Hey! Don't you know that people could hear you?

SIRO. Ha ha ha! What a face—you can read a litany of vice in that face, all right—hyuk hyuk—

LIGURIO. I said, be quiet! I'm sick of you, little man; I really mean it. Now where's Callimaco? (*Callimaco approaches them.*)

CALLIMACO. I'm here! Good to see you fellows—eh?

LIGURIO. Look—keep your servant under control, I think he's a bit crazy; he keeps saying reckless things—now, we don't *want* that!

CALLIMACO. Now Siro, you listen to me. Now you listen here, now. Now you do what he tells you tonight, do you get it?; you do what he says; when he gives you an order, you act the way you do when I give you one, get it? And you keep what you hear, see, and feel to yourself, if you value my money, my honor, my life, and your own welfare, my friend.

SIRO. Yes, master.

CALLIMACO. Did you give the goblet to the professor?

SIRO. Yes, master.

CALLIMACO. What did he say?

SIRO. He said, "Now everything will be in order."

BROTHER TIMOTHY. Is this Callimaco?

CALLIMACO. I am, Father, and at your service.

BROTHER TIMOTHY. And I am ready to do for you that which I wouldn't formerly have done for any man in the world.

CALLIMACO. Your efforts will not be wasted.

BROTHER TIMOTHY. Your love alone is sufficient recompense.

LIGURIO. Please—let's leave these formalities. Siro and I must put on our disguises, and you, Callimaco, must come along too. (*To Brother Timothy.*) We'll be back in two moments.

BROTHER TIMOTHY. I'll be waiting right here. (*Ligurio, Callimaco, and Siro exit.*)

ACT FOUR

SCENE 6

BROTHER TIMOTHY. You know those people who always say, "Bad company leads men to the gallows?" Well, you know— they're right! But sometimes a man is destroyed not through being too selfish or too scheming, but actually through being too accommodating, and eager to help other people. God knows, *I* never thought of hurting anyone in my life; I just stayed in my cell, and came out to recite the appropriate prayers, and occasionally entertained pious men: and then suddenly today this demonic man, this Satan, Ligurio, came into my life, and made me dip my finger into an error, a crime, until my arm was suddenly submerged right up to the shoulder, and now my entire body has followed, and I'm

50

utterly immersed and don't know still what waits for me next. But here comes Ligurio and that sinful valet. (*Ligurio and Siro enter, in disguise.*)

ACT FOUR

SCENE 7

BROTHER TIMOTHY. I'm glad to see you back.
LIGURIO. Do you think we look well?
BROTHER TIMOTHY. Oh, yes—really great.
LIGURIO. Here comes the professor. Oh no! Oh no! (*Nicia enters in disguise and stays at a distance from Ligurio, Siro, and Brother Timothy. He doesn't see them. Ligurio brays with laughter.*)
SIRO. What—you're laughing— ? —
LIGURIO. Haw haw! Oh God—what fun! Say—let's listen— I'll bet he's going to tell about the agonies he's suffered with his wife —haw haw haw!

ACT FOUR

SCENE 8

NICIA. She's peculiar, she's crazy—this affected behavior—these whims, I mean it . . . —Sending the maid to her mother's house, and the servant to the villa—all right, that's fine! But then did she have to subject us to such a scene before getting into bed—those hysterical displays of nausea and dizziness— "I can't! I can't! No please don't make me! Help me! Help me! Oh God, Mother, help me!" —And if her mother hadn't threatened her with the most impious and dangerous incantations, she would never have gotten in between those sheets— (*Pause.*) I hope she develops a really terrible illness—something with a continuous fever that will make her really suffer— (*Pause.*) I like to see women be squeamish about sex—that's just fine, that's wonderful, but not *too* squeamish, because you've driven us insane, you little mouse-brained bitch! And the incredible thing is that if someone were to try to pay her back for all this agony, she'd only say, "But why me? What have I done? What have I done?" (*Pause.*) Well— I'm nicely disguised.

Who would know me? I seem larger, younger, more agile, more active, and there isn't a woman in the city who wouldn't beg me to fuck her for free. — *(Ligurio, Siro, and Brother Timothy approach him.)*

ACT FOUR

SCENE 9

LIGURIO. Good evening, my Lord.

NICIA. Oh! Oh!

LIGURIO. Don't be afraid, Sir— It's only us!

NICIA. Oh! Oh—you're all here? Ha ha! If I hadn't just seen that it was you, I would have run you straight through with this big rapier of mine! Ha! So you're— Ligurio? And you're— Siro? And that other fellow there—oh yes, that's the doctor, eh? Aha ha!

LIGURIO. That's right, my Lord.

NICIA. My goodness! Oh, it's all well-counterfeited, really it is!

LIGURIO. Yes, you see, I've made this one put two nuts in his mouth, so he can't be known by his voice . . .

NICIA. Oh—really—oh really, you *fool*—

LIGURIO. What? Why? I—

NICIA. Why didn't you tell me about that earlier? I could have put nuts in my own mouth as well—you know it's important not to be known by one's speech!

LIGURIO. Well here, take this, put this in your mouth—

NICIA. What's that?

LIGURIO. It's just wax.

NICIA. Well give it here then— Ghaa! —gag—ugh! —shit! —piss!—

LIGURIO. Oh—no—oh really—I'm sorry! I gave you the wrong one there without looking—

NICIA. Shit—piss— What the—what—what—what the—what *was* that?

LIGURIO. That must have been *bitter aloes*, Sir, I guess—you know, that *laxative*— I'm really— I'm terribly sorry—

NICIA. Well go to hell! Piss— Now Doctor, you're not saying a thing—

BROTHER TIMOTHY. I'm just sulking, good Sir, as Ligurio has annoyed me . . . —

NICIA. Ha! Ha! You disguise your voice very well!

LIGURIO. All right now, let's set our ambush right here on this corner. But wait—listen— I think I hear a lute.

NICIA. Good Lord—someone's coming around that corner—what should we do?

LIGURIO. We should send ahead a scout to find out who it is; you go ahead, Siro. You know what to do.

SIRO. Yes— I'm going. (*He exits.*)

NICIA. We can't afford to make a mistake—some dying old man, an invalid! no! —we can't play this game tomorrow night again!

LIGURIO. Don't worry—this Siro's a very good man. (*Siro returns.*)

SIRO. He's just perfect, Sir! Not twenty-five years old, and he's wandering about alone in a shabby little cloak, just playing a lute.

NICIA. Well he sounds just right, if you're telling the truth. Now be careful, it's on your head if we grab this fellow!

SIRO. The boy is just as I've described him, Sir.

NICIA. All right then, Doctor, you stand there; you look the most powerful—oh Lord—here he comes— (*Callimaco enters.*)

CALLIMACO. (*Singing.*)

"May the devil come crawling into your bed
Since I am forbidden to lie there—"

LIGURIO. All right, watch out! Give me that lute.

CALLIMACO. Oh, how frightful! What have I done, Sir?

NICIA. You'll soon find out, boy! Cover his head, gag him!

LIGURIO. Turn him around.

NICIA. One more time! Now put him in the house. (*Siro and Ligurio take Callimaco away.*)

BROTHER TIMOTHY. (*To Nicia.*) My Lord, I think I'm going to lie down for a while; I have a shattering head-ache.

NICIA. That's fine, Doctor—we can easily handle the whole thing ourselves— (*Nicia exits.*)

ACT FOUR

SCENE 10

BROTHER TIMOTHY. Now they're all inside. And now I'll go home too. You know, it's a principle of drama that if the characters sleep in a play, an intermission is required. But we're not having an

53

intermission now, because during this night no one here will sleep. I will say my office. Ligurio and Siro will have supper, because they haven't eaten today. Lord Nicia will wander about his house, from room to room, to make sure that everything is well-dusted and clean and that all is going well. And Lucrezia and Callimaco won't sleep either; at least, I know this, that if I were he, and you were she, —well—we wouldn't sleep, now would we? (*Nymphs and shepherds enter and sing.*)

Oh sweet
night,
oh holy quiet hours
luminous and white
that lie with
desirous
lovers,
in you are joined all joys,
you alone know the secret
of making hearts glad.
Oh night, what dear reward you give
to the amorous ranks
after wearisome battle;
oh happy hours,
you make
every ice-cold breast
to burn with love.

ACT FIVE

SCENE 1

(*Brother Timothy.*)

BROTHER TIMOTHY. I wasn't able to close an eye last night, just thinking and thinking about what was happening. So I did various things to fill the time. I said matins, and I read a life of the Holy Father. I went into the church, and I lit up a lamp that had just gone out. Then I changed the veil on the Virgin Mary, who sometimes does miracles. Lord—how many times I've told the brothers to keep her nice and clean. And then they're amazed that people worship her less often. I remember when there were five hundred little votive images set up on her altar—and now there aren't twenty. And I remember when every single evening we would walk in procession before her, and we had litanies chanted in her praise each Saturday. And we ourselves would make votive offerings there, and in confession we would encourage both women and men always to pray to her too. Now none of these things are done, and the brothers are surprised that people's ardor has grown cold. Oh, the tiny brains, the poor tiny brains of my poor friars— those poor boys— Ah, well— But I hear a great noise in Lord Nicia's house— They're taking out the prisoner! Well well— They obviously waited till the very last drop had come out of the vessel, so to speak; it's already dawn. — (*Ligurio, Siro, Nicia, and Callimaco enter, but do not see Brother Timothy and remain at a distance from him.*)

ACT FIVE

SCENE 2

CALLIMACO. Don't hurt me! Please!
LIGURIO. Get out of here, you moron! (*Callimaco exits.*)
NICIA. Well, he's gone. Let's get ourselves out of these rags. And

why don't you and Siro go find Doctor Callimaco and tell him it all went well?

LIGURIO. But what can we tell him, my friend? We don't know a thing. As soon as we got into the house, we went down to the cellar to drink.

NICIA. Yes, well, that's true. Good Lord—and what good things there are to tell you! Yes, indeed! (Pause.) How should I begin? Well. Well, my wife, of course, was in bed, in the dark. My mother-in-law was waiting by the fire. Then I arrived—with the boy. Well, first I led him around into a pantry beside my main hall; I keep a little lamp in there whose oil has been mixed with some water, so it gives off only a very weak light; I took him in there so that I could examine him without his being able to see my face.

LIGURIO. Hm—very clever—

NICIA. I ordered him to take off his clothes. Well, he hesitated, so I turned in his direction with a sudden quick motion, like an angry dog, like this—and he was so frightened by my gesture— heh heh—that as he hurried to remove his clothes I think it seemed to him as if a thousand years were passing. Then, he stood naked in front of me. (Pause.) He had an ugly face—a grotesque nose, a twisted mouth . . . But when I saw his body—you could never have seen—such beautiful flesh—his skin was so white—it was smooth and soft— And as for certain parts of the boy—you mustn't ask me about those! —

LIGURIO. Well no, we won't need to discuss them, I don't think that we need to discuss those parts— But tell me—was it really necessary to really see—all of the boy in this way? I mean—

NICIA. Well you're joking now, Sir! I mean, once I've put my hands in the dough, my friend, then I really do like to prepare the cake! I mean, I don't do things half-way! We got ourselves this boy; I wanted to see if he was healthy; if he had happened to have had little boils on his skin—little signs of gonorrhea, my friend— then where would I have been? Not examine him! You're joking!

LIGURIO. —well yes—a sensible precaution—

NICIA. When I was sure that he was healthy, I took him along behind me and led him to the bedroom, and then I got him into the bed with my wife. But before I left them, I wanted to feel with my own hands how the experiment was going. You see, it's just not my way to assume that if I look out my window and see a light in my garden, then it means there's a lantern lit there; because that light could be caused by a firefly, you see!

LIGURIO. Yes! Really—you've supervised this business with *such good sense*—

NICIA. I reached under the sheets and felt there—exactly what I'd hoped that I'd feel. Then I left the room, locked the door from the outside, and went to my mother-in-law, who was waiting by the fire, and we spent the whole night engaged in conversation.

LIGURIO. What subjects did your conversation cover, actually?

NICIA. We talked about Lucrezia's thoughtless behavior, and how much better it would have been if she'd agreed to this plan from the first, without hesitations and hysterics. And then we talked about the baby— I felt as if I were already holding him in my arms—the dear little infant child! Suddenly I heard the clock strike five, and, afraid that the day would overtake us, I hurried to the bedroom. What would you say if I told you I couldn't get that weak-witted fellow to wake up?

LIGURIO. Well— I'd believe it.

NICIA. The "greasy pastime" had sated the boy, it appeared! He'd enjoyed his merry-making! Finally, he woke up, I called you, we threw him out, and he was gone—

LIGURIO. It all went so well.

NICIA. Would you believe it if I told you— I really feel *sorry*, you know, for—

LIGURIO. Sorry for what?

NICIA. —for that poor young boy, who has to die so soon because of this—

LIGURIO. Don't worry about the boy. He can worry about himself.

NICIA. Oh yes, I know—it's true. You're right. You're right. (*Pause.*) But goodness, I just can't wait till we can find Doctor Callimaco and have a little *celebration* all around.

LIGURIO. He'll be here outside within an hour, I'm sure. But the day is almost bright. We're off to get out of our costumes. What are you going to do?

NICIA. I'm going to go home and put on some nice, new clothes; then I'll rouse my wife; I'll see to it that she's thoroughly washed; and then I'll take her to church to receive the blessing for expectant mothers. I would like it if you and Doctor Callimaco could be

57

there as well, so that we can all talk to the friar and thank him and reimburse him for all that he's done.

LIGURIO. That's a very good idea. We'll see you at church. For now, *addio*. (*Ligurio, Siro, and Nicia exit.*)

ACT FIVE

SCENE 3

BROTHER TIMOTHY. Well, I overheard that conversation, and I enjoyed every word of it—it was a rare delight to watch the dear old man reach the peak of folly—but the end of the discussion was my favorite part. "Reimbursement"—heh heh—my favorite! That delighted me "beyond all measure," I would say—yes indeed—(*Pause.*) Now they must be going to find me in my cell, but I think I'd prefer to wait for them in church; somehow my wares seem to be worth more there. (*Brother Timothy exits, and Ligurio and Callimaco enter.*)

ACT FIVE

SCENE 4

CALLIMACO. As I told you, my friend, for the first hour I— I felt a kind of terrible nervousness—yes—an unhappiness—my body was in ecstasies—but still I felt sick—I felt awful— But then, after I started to tell her who I was, and I told her that I loved her—that I loved her so much, and then I explained how easily, because of that "simple" quality of her husband, we could live so happily as lovers, without any danger of being discovered, and I promised her that the moment God would arrange other plans for her husband, I would take her as my wife; and then when she had begun to taste all the pleasures I could give her, and she could feel on her lips the difference between a young lover's kisses and those of an elderly husband, she sighed a kind of beautiful sigh, and said: "My Lord, since your cleverness, and the pitiable foolishness of my husband, and my mother's ignorance, and the foul wickedness of my confessor have led me to do that which I myself alone would never have done, I am compelled to believe that it must have been the will of Heaven that it should happen thus; and I am not rash enough, nor have I the strength, to refuse and reject that which Heaven desires me to accept. Therefore I take you as my lord, my master, and my guide. —You are my father. You are my defender. You shall be all my joy. And that which my husband wanted for one night—it is now my desire that he have it forever. You must make yourself his friend, and you must come this morning to church, and from there you must come home to have dinner with him and with me; and the coming and the going in and out of our house will be up to you, and from this moment on you and I will be free at any hour and without any suspicion to meet together and clasp each other in a lover's embrace." — (*Pause.*) Hearing these words, I could have drowned in their sweetness. I couldn't answer her with even the smallest part of what I was feeling, I was so filled with wondrous, overflowing rapture. In short— I find myself the happiest, the most totally happy man that has ever been in the world; and if this happiness doesn't leave me, either through death or time, I shall be more blessed than the blessed, holier than the holy.

LIGURIO. I derive great pleasure from all your joy—and it all happened exactly as I told you it would. But what should we do now?

CALLIMACO. Let's go to the church, because I promised her I'd be there, and that's where she and her mother and her husband can all be met. (*Ligurio and Callimaco exit, and Nicia, Lucrezia, and Sostrata enter.*)

ACT FIVE

SCENE 5

NICIA. Lucrezia— I believe it would be good to do these things in fear of the Lord, and not like an insane person.

LUCREZIA. Well tell me how I'm supposed to behave, then.

NICIA. Listen to the way she answers me! I find her rather bold today, rather cocky, Mother—

SOSTRATA. Well—don't be too surprised by this, Son—she's a little *altered* today—a bit excited—er—

LUCREZIA. But what are you saying?

NICIA. I was saying that I think it would be good if I went on ahead and spoke to the friar, so I can tell him that he should meet you at the door of the church so that you may be led in to receive the blessing for expectant mothers, because, you see, dear, it's really as if you'd been *re-born* today—

LUCREZIA. Well why don't you go then?

NICIA. You're behaving a bit—ha ha—*wildly* this morning, now aren't you, darling? Why, only yesterday afternoon she seemed half dead—

LUCREZIA. This is by your grace, my Lord. (*Brother Timothy enters.*)

ACT FIVE

Scene 6

BROTHER TIMOTHY. You are all most welcome—and may it be granted to you by God, Madonna, to give birth to a lovely male child.

LUCREZIA. If God wills it.

BROTHER TIMOTHY. Well, He certainly will will it, my dear, I *believe*—heh heh— (*Ligurio, Callimaco, and Siro enter.*)

CALLIMACO. (*To Nicia.*) God save you, Sir!

NICIA. Doctor, kindly extend your hand to Lucrezia, my wife—

CALLIMACO. Whoops—with pleasure—

NICIA. Lucrezia, this man will be the cause of our having one day soon a cane on which we may lean in our declining years.

LUCREZIA. I hold him very dear, and I want him to be our most intimate companion and our bosom friend.

NICIA. Now, blessed be you, my dear. How loving of you—how sweet— I'm pleased. And I want him and Ligurio to come home this morning to dine with us.

LUCREZIA. Yes, by all means.

NICIA. And I want to give them the key to that ground-floor room that opens onto the terrace, so that they can lodge themselves there whenever they like, because they have no women at home, and they really live just like poor beasts.

CALLIMACO. I will accept this key, Sir, to use when the occasion arises.

BROTHER TIMOTHY. And I will accept the money for alms.

NICIA. You know full well, Father, how today I will send it to you.

LIGURIO. And is there not anyone here who remembers Siro's great merit?

NICIA. He needs only to ask; what I have is his. But tell me, Lucrezia, how much money do you have with you to give to the friar for being blessed?

LUCREZIA. I don't remember.

NICIA. Ha ha—really—how much now, dear?

LUCREZIA. Oh— I'm so sorry— I forgot all my change. But you can give him some pennies, can't you, my sweet?

NICIA. I'm sick— I don't feel well—don't feel well—

BROTHER TIMOTHY. And you, Madonna Sostrata, in my opinion you've been growing some new shoots on that old trunk of yours—you're really looking well!

SOSTRATA. Who wouldn't be happy at such a time as this?

BROTHER TIMOTHY. Let's all go into the church, and there we'll say the appropriate prayer. Then after the office, you can all go to Lord Nicia's house and dine at your leisure. As for you, dear audience, don't wait for us to come out again: the office is long; and then— I shall stay in the church, and the others will leave by the side door and go to their dinner. So you go home too. Good night to all, and may you all be well.

END

A note to those planning to put on the play, regarding the Wilford Leach production at Joseph Papp's Public Theater.

As you read the play and think about it and work on it, you will eventually come to have your own particular answers to some of the questions that it raises. Do you find Callimaco a sympathetic figure, or is he simply vile and awful? Do you like Ligurio? Do you like Lord Nicia? Is the play a demonstration of an odd political thesis—that dishonesty and manipulation produce happiness on this earth? Or is it on the contrary a bitter sketch of corruption and exploitation, a horrible glimpse into the nature of man (and the relations of men and women)? Or could it best be seen instead as a strange sort of head-long romp through a crumbling world, written by an author who seems to laugh at every single thing that exists under the sun? Or do you perhaps find it a compassionate portrait of struggling humanity? Your view of the play will inevitably be your surest guide to how you want the play to be performed. Now, Wilford Leach's view of it was unique and idiosyncratic and quite unexpected, and, as his production expressed most definitely this very particular view, there were many things in it that you would be most unwise to imitate if your feeling about the play is very different from his. Other things in his production, however, would work just as well in your own, I would think, no matter how you see the play. In any case, his production—which managed to be at the same time both dizzily funny and radiantly lovely—could hardly fail to fascinate anyone interested in the play, and I'm now going to try to describe just a few of its features.

Though frank, unsentimental, and at times quite unpleasant, the Leach production clearly interpreted the play not as an attack on the world and its ways, but rather as a jubilant and unrestrained celebration of life in all its many manifestations. The production seemed somehow an expression of the health and abundance of the Italian Renaissance, and one could glimpse in it some of the same freshness and freedom, and the same sort of luscious, ripe, and generous sensuality, that we see in so many of the paintings of the period. The acting style employed—this is hard to describe—was both subtle and broad, in a way naturalistic and yet at times quite farcical; the characters seemed larger than life, and yet their behavior from moment to moment seemed truthful and believable. No character was played as a caricature. Every actor was sympathetic to the character that he played, and the effect was that the audience felt a sympathy and liking for each one of the people portrayed. The songs were sung in Italian by a single soprano. Lit by a spotlight, singing into a microphone, and wearing an extremely worldly dress, with pink wings on the shoulders, she stood to one side of the stage platform, while on the scenic wall were projected slides of Renaissance paintings with the English translation of the songs superimposed upon them. The music was most delicious—it seemed to meander without strain from thoughtful meditation to cheerful air to languid revery to steamy torch song—and the soprano's singing was delicious too. Thus these interludes between the acts were warm, sensual, and gorgeous, and presented a marked contrast to the sordid and realistically depicted episodes of the play itself. Incidental music—played principally on an RMI (a most versatile electric keyboard instrument)—was used in many scenes throughout the play.

In the Prologue, Machiavelli indicates that the set must depict the Road of Love and at least two doorways, those of Callimaco and Lord Nicia. A church is somewhere in the distance, not too far away. A drop depicting part of a *piazza* and including two doorways would therefore indeed suffice as a minimal set. But the use of such a set would mean that every scene in the play would take place in the public *piazza*, it would also mean that no character in the play could ever sit down. A production using such a set might thus tend to be somewhat formal in style rather than intimate and intense. Leach's solution worked like this: The play was performed in front of a rectangular canvas-on-wood backdrop, on which "The Burning of Savonarola," a Renaissance painting showing the Piazza della Signoria in Florence, had been painstakingly copied by an artist. The backdrop appeared at first to be a solid surface, but in fact two rectangular sections of it, one on each side, were hinged like doors and could open in toward the backstage area to allow the passage of people or objects. These two sections were three feet wide and rose almost eleven feet from the floor. The entire painting, then, stood on a small square platform, into which was set a large circular revolving disk. The platform rested on the floor of the room in which the play was performed; it was twenty feet across and twenty feet deep, and it stood a few inches off the floor. The disk, set in the center of the platform, had a diameter of sixteen feet; the painting which formed the scenic wall was approximately twelve feet from the front of the platform, so the playing area was twenty feet by twelve feet. Three wooden structures—tall but very narrow—served to represent Callimaco's house, Nicia's house, and the church. These, constructed so that they could fit through the narrow openings, consisted in each case of a practical door and doorway, set in a miniaturized suggestion of the surrounding building. When the wall opened, and one of these "buildings" was revolved onto the stage, and when the characters then proceeded to walk through the practical door, the illusion was created that they were then "inside" the building. Appropriate lighting helped to maintain the illusion, although the *piazza*, with the bodies of Savonarola and two others just about to be burned on a huge pyre, was clearly visible throughout the play, as was appropriate. II.2 and II.6, in which Callimaco is the doctor, could thus both be played "indoors," and the characters were also seated, as chairs were revolved onto the stage along with the "house." The crucial scene in which Brother Timothy confronts Lucrezia, III.11, was also played seated and "inside" the church; a few simple elements—some organ music in the background, a Multi-Vox (a device like an Echo-plex) to create the echoing sound of a large church, and a few candles—helped to augment the effect. A "trattoria" in the *piazza* was created by revolving onstage a table and chairs while playing mandolin music in the background; a waiter was employed to bring on food and wine and the check (which Ligurio somehow always managed to have someone else pay). Many of the crucial scenes were played in this "trattoria"—I.2, III.2, III.4, III.8, IV.2, V.2, and V.4. As Act IV was done in moonlight, the "trattoria" table in IV.2 had on it a small glass with a candle inside.

Costuming *The Mandrake* presented problems similar to those that arise when costumes ·are to be selected for any "classical" play. To begin with what is obvious: the story of *The Mandrake*, in its assumptions, broad outlines, and tiny details, makes sense in sixteenth century Florence; it doesn't make sense in any other period. An audience can believe that a sixteenth century Florentine lover might just possibly impersonate a doctor by speaking in Latin and prescribing a mandrake potion; but an audience would not believe that a lover in New York City would do this today; nor would they believe that a lover in Edwardian London would do it. For this reason, to have costumed the play in the style of any incorrect period—including our own—would have tended to make the play unbelievable. But to have costumed the play in accurate sixteenth century Florentine style would have presented a different but equally disturbing problem. Unfortunate as this may be, it happens to be a fact that a contemporary audience simply has no idea how to interpret the clothing of any distant place or time. They simply do not know whether a particular sort of sixteenth century collar, sleeve, or cuff indicates wealth or poverty, arrogance or modesty, good taste or bad taste. So they can learn little or nothing about the characters they are observing from seeing them in such costumes. And in fact they can't help *mis*-reading these costumes—and their most serious mistake will be that they will be unable to believe that people dressed so differently from themselves can really be anything *like* themselves. And if they feel that the characters *aren't* like themselves, they won't identify themselves with the characters, and thus they will remain unmoved by their joys and sorrows, and unexcited by the play. Furthermore, confronted by a stage full of people in incomprehensible costumes, meaningless to them, an audience may feel in an odd way betrayed by the creators of the spectacle they are watching and doubtful about its purpose: are they really being told a story that has some relationship to their own lives, they may wonder, or are they instead being taught some sort of lesson about history? Do the producers of this play really want them to be gripped and fascinated by it—as audiences were when it was done in its own period—or do they have some peculiar motive for wanting them to have a somewhat *less* compelling experience?

Leach and the costume designer, Patricia McGourty, solved the problem for *The Mandrake* by setting the play in a made-up period. The costumes were designed to fit so naturally and pleasingly into the sixteenth century backdrop that they gave no impression of clashing eras; the audience felt that they were watching life being lived in the Italian Renaissance. But in fact the costumes used fragments from the clothing styles of many twentieth century periods as well as the sixteenth century, in order to convey, in the most direct manner, the essential nature of every character. Thus Ligurio looked something like a contemporary lower-class Italian con man, perhaps out of a film by Fellini: his costume consisted of black alligator Italian shoes, orange herring-bone trousers, an orange satin collarless cowboy shirt with a black ruff, and a green satin smoking jacket. The smoking jacket's sleeves were laced on, which created an impression of resourceful penuriousness, but which also carried a suggestion of the sixteenth century; also, he wore blue velvet arm garters with black beading and flowers, which conveyed a sixteenth century feeling as well, but also suggested some sort of fast-living saloon piano-player of the early twentieth century. He also wore a Saint Christopher medal and cross on a chain around his neck. Callimaco wore a red and green rugby shirt with a tan turtleneck underneath and a ruff coming out from the turtleneck. He also wore brown dress shoes, tan trousers, and a long red and white striped college scarf. Madonna Sostrata looked something like a Marie Dressler or Margaret Dumont figure from an early movie. She wore a black beaded 1920's dress with a red-cut velvet train; over this she had on a trailing chiffon evening coat trimmed in black feathers, with a large deep-red rose corsage. She also wore a wide-brimmed pink feathered hat, veiled in black.

A few deliberately and outrageously anachronistic touches were used in the production, both to make it unmistakable that the play was about *us today*, however long ago it may have been written, and also in effect as tokens of the good faith of those presenting the performance. The spaghetti eaten by Ligurio, the travel folders he showed to Lord Nicia, the football appliqué on Callimaco's shirt, the Shriners' outfits used as disguises—all contributed to a feeling that Machiavelli's play was being performed precisely because it deals with human life as it still is today; it was not being presented in order to instruct the audience about history or offer it a chance to escape into a falsely harmless, pleasant world of the past. In effect, these anachronisms were like little windows into the *reality* of the play; they helped to make it clear that the characters were to be seen as real people, involved in real situations and tormented by real passions. And they also conveyed the point that those putting *on* the play were alive as well, and shared a world with the audience. The actors and all those associated with the production were actually human beings *themselves*, in other words, and they were trying to have fun and survive and find happiness, like the people in the audience.

A few lines in the play were changed to suit the situation (these are *not* changed in the text in this book); for example, as Ligurio had just eaten a large meal in full view of the audience, Brother Timothy in IV.10 didn't describe him as not having eaten all day. And a few lines were added for various reasons (and these have not been added to the text of this book): for example, "Shall we have something to eat?", "A little wine, Father?" and others as necessary. And certain lines improvised by the actors during rehearsals were also ultimately included in the final production. For example, in III.11, when Brother Timothy said, ". . . it is the will that sins, and not the body," he then always said "Repeat that" and forced the unwilling Lucrezia to repeat it, between her sobs, and when he said, "Indeed, the Bible tells us that the daughters of Lot, believing themselves to be the only women left in the world, actually used their own father for sexual intercourse," Lucrezia always said, "Oh no! Oh no!" and when he went on to say, "but because their purpose was good, they did not sin," Madonna Sostrata always said, "That's interesting." (I haven't included these lines in the text either, naturally, as they have no basis at all in Machiavelli and make sense only in the context of one particular production, and indeed I would caution very strongly against any such improvised lines in general. If injudicious or inappropriate, they can easily destroy an entire scene—or, in fact, the entire play. However, I must admit that my own opinion is that the spirit of the play and the nature of the play—added to the fact that while the original may be a "classic," no translation *can* be one—do permit the very occasional use of such fundamentally dangerous improprieties.)

Another satisfying feature of the Leach production was that in the play's final scene, Callimaco actually gave money to Ligurio and Siro (coins only for Siro), and Lord Nicia gave money to Ligurio and Brother Timothy (he had none left for Siro, despite Ligurio's attempt to procure some for him). All money was changed from ducats to lire, one ducat being equivalent to a million lire (a totally fictitious exchange-rate). Thus "twenty-five ducats" was changed to "twenty-five million lire" and so on throughout the play. The same actor played Siro and the Prologue, and Siro appeared as a silent character in II.2, II.6, V.2, and V.4. Also, the same actress played Madonna Sostrata and the Woman in the Church, and her costumes were planned for a very quick change. A large chart proved quite useful in illuminating Callimaco's discourse on sterility in Latin.

The only major alteration that Leach made in the play was to change Callimaco's age from thirty to twenty (this was done by altering one word of the text). Instead of an experienced roué, Callimaco became a love-sick, mercurial adolescent or student, crazed by sexual frenzy—rather easily duped by the hard-working Ligurio, but dangerous and difficult to control. At times he went berserk, lifted Ligurio off the ground, and seemed prepared to throw him into the Arno, and when impersonating the doctor he fell into fits of wild laughing and erotic revery (at times verging on masturbation), from which Ligurio was obliged constantly to rescue him. This change in Callimaco led to the insertion of a speech by Ligurio to the audience after Callimaco's exit at the end of Act I; this speech, which I was obliged to invent with no help from Machiavelli, went like this: "You know, some people say I don't work for my living. That's really funny, isn't it? And, you know, the people who say this haven't worked a day in their lives. I know, if we survive the next twenty-four hours and it all turns out well, I stand to take in a big pile of money. But if that does happen, I really will have earned it. I mean, it's terrifying to think about it—how am I going to be able to keep that boy under control? He's impossible! And the joke, of course, is that this whole thing is for *his* benefit; but if he does go crazy and the plan is discovered—well—he's a rich boy; maybe he'll get out of it; but I'll be destroyed in this town for sure."

The character of Lucrezia, also, was changed, to the extent that in III.11, the scene with Brother Timothy, her resistance was really quite violent; she cried, screamed, fought—and constantly shouted, "No! I won't! I don't want to do that!"

The production ran just about exactly two hours and was performed without any intermission. (The logical place for an intermission would seem to be at the end of Act III, but it just didn't seem necessary.)

NOTE ON MUSIC

Depending on what sort of production you do, you may wish to set the songs to music in a Renaissance style, a modern style, a popular style, or any combination, and you may wish to use one voice or many voices, a simple guitar or keyboard, or a large ensemble.

In the original New York production, the music was composed by Richard Weinstock. The songs were in Italian and were written for a single soprano voice. The ensemble consisted of three instrumentalists: the first played keyboards (an RMI Rock-Si-Chord stereo output electric keyboard, a key bass machine, and a piano with mandolin bar); the second played guitar, electric guitar, and mandolin; and the third played the tenor and alto recorders, clarinet, flute, alto sax, and chimes. The songs and also all the incidental music are available from Richard Weinstock, % Sumac Music, 1697 Broadway, New York, N.Y. 10019. A piano with tacks will work as well as a piano with mandolin bar, and any electric keyboard with stereo output and stops for organ and harpsichord can be used instead of the RMI. A prose translation of the songs into English, more suitable for projection (as in the New York production) than the verse translation, may be obtained from me: Wallace Shawn, % New York Shakespeare Festival, 425 Lafayette Street, New York, N.Y. 10003.

The songs in English have been set to music by Allen Shawn, for single voice and accompaniment, and this music is also available: Allen Shawn, 284 Hudson Street, New York, N.Y. 10013.

NOTE ON COSTUMES

The costume plot that follows gives an indication of what the original New York production was like. Patricia McGourty's costumes were designed specifically for Wilford Leach's production, and they obviously represent a very special and unusual view of the characters. It will help you to read the costume plot if you think in terms of certain models: For Prologue and Siro: a down-trodden author; for Callimaco: Harold Lloyd; for Ligurio: a lower-class Italian con man out of Fellini; for Nicia: a cross between Wallace Beery and Charles Ruggles; for Sostrata: Marie Dressler or Margaret Dumont; for the Woman in the Church: an earthy peasant; for Lucrezia: Walt Disney's Cinderella.

PROPERTY LIST

Glass urinal

Money (Nicia)

Money (Callimaco)

Coins (Woman)

Silver goblet, with cloth to cover it

Nuts (Brother Timothy)

Aloes (Ligurio)

Lute (Callimaco)

COSTUME PLOT

SIRO:
Doctor coat
Beige corduroy trousers
Maroon and gold suspenders
Brown turtleneck sweater
Beige cardigan sweater
Maroon and beige mesh scarf
Brown wool socks
Brown slip on shoes
Maroon satin cape and fez

CALLIMACO (Think of Harold Lloyd):
Beige trousers
Cream turtleneck sweater
Red and green striped T-shirt with ¾ sleeves and football applique
Red, maroon and white stripe scarf
Detachable ruff
Beige socks
Brown Italian lace up shoes
Flesh colored underwear
White jockey shorts
Disguise trimmed with fishing ropes and seashells
Brown felt hat
Beige cape
Doctor coat

LIGURIO (Think of an Italian film con man):
Rust trousers
Khaki green suspenders
Orange satin cowboy shirt
Green jacket with tie-on sleeves
Blue sleeve garter with jet trim and roses
Orange print handkerchief
Neckchain with cross and medal
Black socks with red stripes
Black alligator shoes
Orange satin cape
Fez

NICIA (Think of a cross between Wallace Beery and Charles Ruggles):
Jodphurs
Beige shirt
Brown belt
Black ascot with white dots
Green tie pin
Burgundy velvet smoking jacket with black academic sleeves
Black beret with medallion
Handkerchief with brown stripes
Red and green academic hood
Riding boots
Glasses with round tortoise frames
Rhinestone ring
Gold cufflinks
Red satin cape
Fez

MADONNA SOSTRATA (Think of Marie Dressler or Margaret Dumont):
Black beaded twenties dress
Maroon train (detachable)
Black chiffon cloak trimmed with maribou
Pink straw picture hat with pink and white feathers, black veil
Maroon elbow length gloves
Black beaded bag
Black hose and high heeled sandals

PEASANT LADY:
Grey underdress with attached pink overskirt, lavender shawl; at waist,
    orange apron
Black mantilla
Grey low wedgie sandals

BROTHER TIMOTHY:
Black cassock
Black trousers
Dickey with attached celluloid collar
Black sash
Rosary and lavender rhinestone cross
Little priest hat with pompom
Black jazz shoes
Black socks
Alb
Burgundy velour cape
Black fez
Black cape

LUCREZIA (Think of Walt Disney's Cinderella):
Pink lace slip
Pink chiffon dress with train
Hose
Beaded necklace
Beige shoes with pink roses
Flowered braid
Wedding ring
White mantilla
Handkerchief

ACT V

Lavender lace and beaded dress
Pink and lavender chiffon overjacket
Lavender pumps
Flower and pearl head piece
Pearl earrings

SINGER:
Green dress with lace sleeves and pink wings
Green shoes

WAITER:
Green corduroy trousers
Green turtleneck sweater
Detachable ruff
Black vest
Yellow stripe apron
Black shoes
Yellow bandanna

MUSICIANS:
All wear rust turtlenecks
Detachable ruffs

NEW PLAYS

★ **GUARDIANS by Peter Morris.** In this unflinching look at war, a disgraced American soldier discloses the truth about Abu Ghraib prison, and a clever English journalist reveals how he faked a similar story for the London tabloids. "Compelling, sympathetic and powerful." –*NY Times.* "Sends you into a state of moral turbulence." –*Sunday Times (UK).* "Nothing short of remarkable." –*Village Voice.* [1M, 1W] ISBN: 978-0-8222-2177-7

★ **BLUE DOOR by Tanya Barfield.** Three generations of men (all played by one actor), from slavery through Black Power, challenge Lewis, a tenured professor of mathematics, to embark on a journey combining past and present. "A teasing flare for words." –*Village Voice.* "Unfailingly thought-provoking." –*LA Times.* "The play moves with the speed and logic of a dream." –*Seattle Weekly.* [2M] ISBN: 978-0-8222-2209-5

★ **THE INTELLIGENT DESIGN OF JENNY CHOW by Rolin Jones.** This irreverent "techno-comedy" chronicles one brilliant woman's quest to determine her heritage and face her fears with the help of her astounding creation called Jenny Chow. "Boldly imagined." –*NY Times.* "Fantastical and funny." –*Variety.* "Harvests many laughs and finally a few tears." –*LA Times.* [3M, 3W] ISBN: 978-0-8222-2071-8

★ **SOUVENIR by Stephen Temperley.** Florence Foster Jenkins, a wealthy society eccentric, suffers under the delusion that she is a great coloratura soprano—when in fact the opposite is true. "Hilarious and deeply touching. Incredibly moving and breathtaking." –*NY Daily News.* "A sweet love letter of a play." –*NY Times.* "Wildly funny. Completely charming." –*Star-Ledger.* [1M, 1W] ISBN: 978-0-8222-2157-9

★ **ICE GLEN by Joan Ackermann.** In this touching period comedy, a beautiful poetess dwells in idyllic obscurity on a Berkshire estate with a band of unlikely cohorts. "A beautifully written story of nature and change." –*Talkin' Broadway.* "A lovely play which will leave you with a lot to think about." –*CurtainUp.* "Funny, moving and witty." –*Metroland (Boston).* [4M, 3W] ISBN: 978-0-8222-2175-3

★ **THE LAST DAYS OF JUDAS ISCARIOT by Stephen Adly Guirgis.** Set in a time-bending, darkly comic world between heaven and hell, this play reexamines the plight and fate of the New Testament's most infamous sinner. "An unforced eloquence that finds the poetry in lowdown street talk." –*NY Times.* "A real jaw-dropper." –*Variety.* "An extraordinary play." –*Guardian (UK).* [10M, 5W] ISBN: 978-0-8222-2082-4

DRAMATISTS PLAY SERVICE, INC.
440 Park Avenue South, New York, NY 10016 212-683-8960 Fax 212-213-1539
postmaster@dramatists.com www.dramatists.com

NEW PLAYS

★ **THE GREAT AMERICAN TRAILER PARK MUSICAL music and lyrics by David Nehls, book by Betsy Kelso.** Pippi, a stripper on the run, has just moved into Armadillo Acres, wreaking havoc among the tenants of Florida's most exclusive trailer park. "Adultery, strippers, murderous ex-boyfriends, Costco and the Ice Capades. Undeniable fun." *–NY Post.* "Joyful and unashamedly vulgar." *–The New Yorker.* "Sparkles with treasure." *–New York Sun.* [2M, 5W] ISBN: 978-0-8222-2137-1

★ **MATCH by Stephen Belber.** When a young Seattle couple meet a prominent New York choreographer, they are led on a fraught journey that will change their lives forever. "Uproariously funny, deeply moving, enthralling theatre." *–NY Daily News.* "Prolific laughs and ear-to-ear smiles." *–NY Magazine.* [2M, 1W] ISBN: 978-0-8222-2020-6

★ **MR. MARMALADE by Noah Haidle.** Four-year-old Lucy's imaginary friend, Mr. Marmalade, doesn't have much time for her—not to mention he has a cocaine addiction and a penchant for pornography. "Alternately hilarious and heartbreaking." *–The New Yorker.* "A mature and accomplished play." *–LA Times.* "Scathingly observant comedy." *–Miami Herald.* [4M, 2W] ISBN: 978-0-8222-2142-5

★ **MOONLIGHT AND MAGNOLIAS by Ron Hutchinson.** Three men cloister themselves as they work tirelessly to reshape a screenplay that's just not working—*Gone with the Wind.* "Consumers of vintage Hollywood insider stories will eat up Hutchinson's diverting conjecture." *–Variety.* "A lot of fun." *–NY Post.* "A Hollywood dream-factory farce." *–Chicago Sun-Times.* [3M, 1W] ISBN: 978-0-8222-2084-8

★ **THE LEARNED LADIES OF PARK AVENUE by David Grimm, translated and freely adapted from Molière's Les Femmes Savantes.** Dicky wants to marry Betty, but her mother's plan is for Betty to wed a most pompous man. "A brave, brainy and barmy revision." *–Hartford Courant.* "A rare but welcome bird in contemporary theatre." *–New Haven Register.* "Roll over Cole Porter." *–Boston Globe.* [5M, 5W] ISBN: 978-0-8222-2135-7

★ **REGRETS ONLY by Paul Rudnick.** A sparkling comedy of Manhattan manners that explores the latest topics in marriage, friendships and squandered riches. "One of the funniest quip-meisters on the planet." *–NY Times.* "Precious moments of hilarity. Devastatingly accurate political and social satire." *–BackStage.* "Great fun." *–CurtainUp.* [3M, 3W] ISBN: 978-0-8222-2223-1

DRAMATISTS PLAY SERVICE, INC.
440 Park Avenue South, New York, NY 10016 212-683-8960 Fax 212-213-1539
postmaster@dramatists.com www.dramatists.com

NEW PLAYS

★ **AFTER ASHLEY by Gina Gionfriddo.** A teenager is unwillingly thrust into the national spotlight when a family tragedy becomes talk-show fodder. "A work that virtually any audience would find accessible." *–NY Times.* "Deft characterization and caustic humor." *–NY Sun.* "A smart satirical drama." *–Variety.* [4M, 2W] ISBN: 978-0-8222-2099-2

★ **THE RUBY SUNRISE by Rinne Groff.** Twenty-five years after Ruby struggles to realize her dream of inventing the first television, her daughter faces similar battles of faith as she works to get Ruby's story told on network TV. "Measured and intelligent, optimistic yet clear-eyed." *–NY Magazine.* "Maintains an exciting sense of ingenuity." *–Village Voice.* "Sinuous theatrical flair." *–Broadway.com.* [3M, 4W] ISBN: 978-0-8222-2140-1

★ **MY NAME IS RACHEL CORRIE taken from the writings of Rachel Corrie, edited by Alan Rickman and Katharine Viner.** This solo piece tells the story of Rachel Corrie who was killed in Gaza by an Israeli bulldozer set to demolish a Palestinian home. "Heartbreaking urgency. An invigoratingly detailed portrait of a passionate idealist." *–NY Times.* "Deeply authentically human." *–USA Today.* "A stunning dramatization." *–CurtainUp.* [1W] ISBN: 978-0-8222-2222-4

★ **ALMOST, MAINE by John Cariani.** A cast of Mainers (or "Mainiacs" if you prefer) fall in and out of love in ways that only people who live in close proximity to wild moose can do. "A whimsical approach to the joys and perils of romance." *–NY Times.* "Sweet, poignant and witty." *–NY Daily News.* "John Cariani aims for the heart by way of the funny bone." *–Star-Ledger.* [2M, 2W] ISBN: 978-0-8222-2156-2

★ **Mitch Albom's TUESDAYS WITH MORRIE by Jeffrey Hatcher and Mitch Albom, based on the book by Mitch Albom.** The true story of Brandeis University professor Morrie Schwartz and his relationship with his student Mitch Albom. "A touching, life-affirming, deeply emotional drama." *–NY Daily News.* "You'll laugh. You'll cry." *–Variety.* "Moving and powerful." *–NY Post.* [2M] ISBN: 978-0-8222-2188-3

★ **DOG SEES GOD: CONFESSIONS OF A TEENAGE BLOCKHEAD by Bert V. Royal.** An abused pianist and a pyromaniac ex-girlfriend contribute to the teen-angst of America's most hapless kid. "A welcome antidote to the notion that the *Peanuts* gang provides merely American cuteness." *–NY Times.* "Hysterically funny." *–NY Post.* "The *Peanuts* kids have finally come out of their shells." *–Time Out.* [4M, 4W] ISBN: 978-0-8222-2152-4

DRAMATISTS PLAY SERVICE, INC.
440 Park Avenue South, New York, NY 10016 212-683-8960 Fax 212-213-1539
postmaster@dramatists.com   www.dramatists.com

NEW PLAYS

★ **RABBIT HOLE by David Lindsay-Abaire.** Winner of the 2007 Pulitzer Prize. Becca and Howie Corbett have everything a couple could want until a life-shattering accident turns their world upside down. "An intensely emotional examination of grief, laced with wit." *—Variety.* "A transcendent and deeply affecting new play." *—Entertainment Weekly.* "Painstakingly beautiful." *—BackStage.* [2M, 3W] ISBN: 978-0-8222-2154-8

★ **DOUBT, A Parable by John Patrick Shanley.** Winner of the 2005 Pulitzer Prize and Tony Award. Sister Aloysius, a Bronx school principal, takes matters into her own hands when she suspects the young Father Flynn of improper relations with one of the male students. "All the elements come invigoratingly together like clockwork." *—Variety.* "Passionate, exquisite, important, engrossing." *—NY Newsday.* [1M, 3W] ISBN: 978-0-8222-2219-4

★ **THE PILLOWMAN by Martin McDonagh.** In an unnamed totalitarian state, an author of horrific children's stories discovers that someone has been making his stories come true. "A blindingly bright black comedy." *—NY Times.* "McDonagh's least forgiving, bravest play." *—Variety.* "Thoroughly startling and genuinely intimidating." *—Chicago Tribune.* [4M, 5 bit parts (2M, 1W, 1 boy, 1 girl)] ISBN: 978-0-8222-2100-5

★ **GREY GARDENS book by Doug Wright, music by Scott Frankel, lyrics by Michael Korie.** The hilarious and heartbreaking story of Big Edie and Little Edie Bouvier Beale, the eccentric aunt and cousin of Jacqueline Kennedy Onassis, once bright names on the social register who became East Hampton's most notorious recluses. "An experience no passionate theatergoer should miss." *—NY Times.* "A unique and unmissable musical." *—Rolling Stone.* [4M, 3W, 2 girls] ISBN: 978-0-8222-2181-4

★ **THE LITTLE DOG LAUGHED by Douglas Carter Beane.** Mitchell Green could make it big as the hot new leading man in Hollywood if Diane, his agent, could just keep him in the closet. "Devastatingly funny." *—NY Times.* "An out-and-out delight." *—NY Daily News.* "Full of wit and wisdom." *—NY Post.* [2M, 2W] ISBN: 978-0-8222-2226-2

★ **SHINING CITY by Conor McPherson.** A guilt-ridden man reaches out to a therapist after seeing the ghost of his recently deceased wife. "Haunting, inspired and glorious." *—NY Times.* "Simply breathtaking and astonishing." *—Time Out.* "A thoughtful, artful, absorbing new drama." *—Star-Ledger.* [3M, 1W] ISBN: 978-0-8222-2187-6

DRAMATISTS PLAY SERVICE, INC.
440 Park Avenue South, New York, NY 10016 212-683-8960 Fax 212-213-1539
postmaster@dramatists.com www.dramatists.com